Because of his faith and generosity, David Green has changed the world. His love and friendship have changed our ministry. His story will change your walk with God.

—Dr. David Jeremiah, founder and president, Turning Point Ministries

If you want to be smart, you find out what smart people do and imitate that. And I've known David Green long enough to understand that he is worth imitating. His business wisdom is surpassed only by his integrity and faith. This book reflects David at his very best.

—Dave Ramsey, bestselling author and nationally syndicated radio show host

By any measure, David Green is a successful businessman. But much more important, David is a faithful man and a generous man, because he sees life with an eternal perspective. He understands that God entrusts us with his resources to do his work here on earth, for the purposes of heaven. This is an inspiring and challenging book that has the potential to change the way you look at everything you do.

—Jim Daly, president, Focus on the Family

David Green has lived out his true calling to lead a company owned by God and for God's glory. The way of living generously comes from humble life lessons. David not only learned these critical lessons but applies them daily in all aspects of his life.

—Terence Chatmon, president and CEO, Fellowship of Companies for Christ International

I am honored to give my unreserved endorsement to this wonderful book! I believe it will become a classic and treasured work and an inspiration for countless others. I read it with great joy and will recommend it to our team and members as soon as it is available.

—Buck Jacobs, founder, C12 Group

David Green's new book is hands down the most amazing story about giving I've ever read. Get ready to be blessed as you read this power-packed book sure to inspire you to embrace a life of extravagant generosity.

—Craig Groeschel, pastor, Life.Church; author, *Divine Direction: Seven Decisions That Will Change Your Life*

We tend to overestimate what we can achieve in short periods of time and underestimate what God can do with a man or woman over a lifetime. Look at the principles, lessons, disciplines, and results of David Green's life and be inspired to trust God!

—Dr. Roy L. Peterson, president and CEO, American Bible Society

This is a landmark book on the delight and joy of generous giving. May it ignite a massive movement of lavish generosity with eternity in view! David Green gets it. (And he gives it away!)

—Dick Eastman, international president, Every Home for Christ

This book is a compelling case for radical generosity borne out of personal experience. Read it. It is practical, inspiring, and challenging.

—J. Frank Harrison III, chairman and CEO, Coca-Cola Bottling Co. Consolidated

This book lays out tested biblical principles for family legacy and wealth management based on real life examples from the Green family. Your business and your family will be the beneficiaries of their strong thinking.

—Greg Leith, CEO, Convene

David Green's remarkable story of building a business and then making its assets available to the kingdom of God involves an unswerving commitment of stewardship over the wealth God has entrusted to him. This book will inspire you to do as Jesus said: "Seek first his kingdom."

—Dr. George O. Wood, general superintendent, General Council of the Assemblies of God

David Green shares the biblical principles that guide his family's radical generosity. Candid and compelling, this book will change the way you look at your possessions and inspire you to believe God for opportunities to give more away.

—Hal Donaldson, president, Convoy of Hope, Inc.

I can think of few people living out the idea of biblical generosity like David. The values expressed in this book are timeless because they are biblical. I commend this book to all seeking to leave their family's legacy for generations to come.

—Chris Holdorf, CEO, National Christian Foundation

This book shares one man's story of learning to live with an open hand and the blessings of a God who is faithful and extravagantly generous. You will find wisdom that comes from walking in everyday decisions that lead to the peace and security of God's plan to give it all away.

—Lee Truax, president, CBMC, Inc.

Wealth is found in our families through the values transferred from one generation to the next. David Green has demonstrated not only to his own family but to the family of believers worldwide how we can all be truly wealthy only by giving it all away.

—Paul Weber, president and CEO, Family Policy Alliance

I've long known of the Green family and their extraordinary generosity. I also know that when a man like David Green writes a book, I want to read it cover to cover.

—Rev. Samuel Rodriguez, president, National Hispanic Christian Leadership Conference

To me, David Green is truly a hero of the faith. It is a privilege to recommend this book, which reflects the proper perspective on stewarding what God has entrusted to each of us. May each of us follow his example.

—Ron Blue, founder, Kingdom Advisors

David Green has publicly taken courageous moral stands with Hobby Lobby, a company he founded, but which he knows belongs to God. I loved this wonderful book of wise and integrity-permeated perspectives on God-honoring values in the workplace, enduring family legacies, and the heartfelt joy and enduring rewards of giving.

—Randy Alcorn, author, *Heaven* and *The Treasure Principle*

GIVING IT ALL AWAY . . .

AND GETTING IT ALL BACK AGAIN

The Way of Living Generously

DAVID GREEN

with BILL HIGH

ZONDERVAN®

ZONDERVAN

Giving It All Away... and Getting It All Back Again

Requests for information should be addressed to:
Zondervan, 3900 Sparks Dr. SE, Grand Rapids, Michigan 49546

Zondervan titles may be purchased in bulk for educational, business, fundraising, or promotional use. For information, please email SpecialMarkets@Zondervan.com.

ISBN 978-0-310-34794-1 (hardcover)
ISBN 978-0-310-34952-5 (international trade paper edition)
ISBN 978-0-310-34796-5 (audio)
ISBN 978-0-310-34795-8 (ebook)

Author is represented by the Christopher Ferebee Agency, www.ChristopherFerebee.com.

Cover design: Darren Welch Design
Cover illustration: © Gizele/Shutterstock®
Interior design: Denise Froehlich

Printed in the United States of America

20 21 22 23 24 25 PC/LSCC 15 14 13 12 11 10

To my grandchildren and their spouses, Brent and Trang Green, Tyler and Kristin Green, Scott Green, Joe and Amy Fallon, Derek and Erica Green, Lauren and Michael McAfee, Lindy Green, Caleb and Danielle Smith, Grace Green, and Gabi Green: you are a great joy to my life.

To my eleven great-grandchildren and the great-grandchildren who are still to come: may you continue in the legacy of faithfulness that your parents have set before you.

CONTENTS

FOREWORD

I AM SO HONORED to be allowed a brief say at the beginning of this tremendous book by someone I admire to an almost embarrassing extent that I could just about bust. If you need to read that sentence again, please feel free. But it's true: my appreciation for the Green family—and what their example means in a world that desperately needs such examples—and for David Green in particular is unbounded.

And I'm certain that this book will help you see exactly what I mean.

The real joy of reading this book, and in some ways the funniest thing about it, is that it will not fail to get you excited—or at the very least at peace—about the two things in life that are often dreaded and that are famously said to be inevitable: death and taxes. I'm not kidding. When you read the book, you'll see. (Actually, you're already reading the book, so just keep going!)

David Green helps us see what he sees so clearly: that the world we live in is only temporary, and that in the short space we have while we are here, we have the inestimable and glorious opportunity to use whatever we have to do eternal things. Imagine that! I have no idea how David Green has conveyed this vital truth so powerfully, but he has. Simply by telling the story of his life and sharing some anecdotes, he makes the reader look forward to joining the spectacular adventure that he and his family have been on for three generations and counting. And yes, we really do get to join the adventure! And David Green makes it clear that he isn't selling hope; he is just telling the truth. The God he serves is real, and what God says, is really true, and we can take that to the bank. Literally and figuratively and any other way you can think of.

One more thing that I must convey before I run off to get the subway: I've had the genuine privilege of getting to know the Greens, and the impossible-but-true fact is that the older they are, the younger they are. When I met David and his wife, Barbara, who are the patriarch and matriarch of this extraordinary multigeneration clan, I hardly expected to meet a pair of supervibrant, superfun people who seemed somehow to be younger than their children and grandchildren. They were the oldest chronologically, but they were the youngest in every other way. Which helped me come to see that the longer you walk with God, the younger you get. That's the way it's supposed to work. It's the paradox of the kingdom of heaven. And by walking, I don't just mean sauntering along with God absentmindedly, but really walking with him intentionally. Because the more intensely you walk with him in all your ways, the more he imparts his eternal newness and youth to you.

So if you really give yourself over to walking with the Lord of Lords, at some point you just begin to glow. That's the only explanation I can give for the Green G1 generation, as they call themselves. And then at some point eventually, I suppose you get to where your glow is so bright that it's just impossible to reconcile with this world of shadows, and that's the point at which the Lord opens the door to glory, which is a place where they can handle your brightness better, because they're even brighter than you are. I don't think I've ever looked more forward to getting older and dying, but by reading this book and knowing how things are really supposed to work, you just can't help it. That's the crazy and unbridled joy of really walking with the God of the Bible, and in reading this book you will be walking with him because you'll be walking with those who are walking with him.

So now I'll step aside so you can enjoy what I have enjoyed. God bless you as you read! And he will.

—Eric Metaxas, New York City, January 2017

PROLOGUE

The questions are different at different stages of life.

In our twenties we tend to ask, "Who will I marry and what will my career be?" In our thirties we start to ask, "How can I be established in my career, and how will my kids turn out?"

By the forties we start to ask, "Is this the job I really wanted, and why is life so hard?" In our fifties we start to look both backward and forward: "How has it turned out so far, and what will I do that's significant in the next twenty-five years?"

By our sixties, we ask simpler questions like, "Will my health hold out, and when will I see my grandchildren?" By our seventies and eighties, we really start to look back and ask, "Was it all worth it, or will anyone remember?" We might even ask, "Should I have, could I have, given more?"

The funny thing about the questions of life is that the ones we ask at the end are the ones we should begin with. It is tough to craft a meaningful life without considering our end: What do we hope for, what do we dream for, relative to our lives, our family, our children?

My hope is that this book will bring some of those questions to the forefront for you. That it will raise new questions and examine old questions from new vantage points.

In particular, I hope that some of the questions that we put off—about our mortality, about our sense of meaning and success—we can begin to address right now. And that we'll find we are talking not about endings but about enduring legacies.

Part 1

A RADICAL WAY OF LIVING

Many [Western Christians] habitually think and act as if there is no eternity. We major in the momentary and minor in the momentous.

—RANDY ALCORN

Giving frees us from the familiar territory of our own needs by opening our mind to the unexplained worlds occupied by the needs of others.

—BARBARA BUSH

Give, and it will be given to you. Good measure, pressed down, shaken together, running over, will be put into your lap. For with the measure you use it will be measured back to you.

—JESUS OF NAZARETH

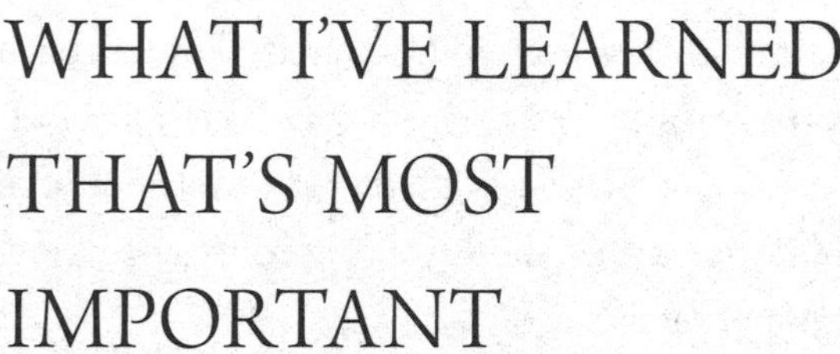

Chapter 1

WHAT I'VE LEARNED THAT'S MOST IMPORTANT

The only way to know the strength of God is to take the yoke of Jesus upon us and to learn from him.

—Oswald Chambers, Evangelist and Teacher

People walk into our Hobby Lobby stores, stores that cover anywhere from thirty-five thousand to seventy thousand square feet and carry every kind of craft that we see as helpful, fun, and useful in a home setting. You see furniture and fabrics, empty frames, and frames filled with canvassed fine art prints and metal art, home decor like candles and lights and lamps, art supplies with easels and tubes of oils and acrylic and watercolors and brushes—and this store is replicated seven hundred times across this country.

This is the enjoyable part of running a national company. But there can be an unpleasant side to this growth and success, a side that puts one in the public eye in undesirable ways.

For example, suing the federal government is a great way to attract a lot of unwanted attention. That's particularly true when your case goes all the way to the United States Supreme Court and makes all kinds of national news.

Now, to be clear, we never sought this. In the following pages, you'll read that we started from pretty humble beginnings. I picked cotton. We started our business out of our home in 1970. Even as our business grew, we always attempted to stay out of the limelight. But there are times when the test of your conscience is greater than the test of your pocketbook.

By way of background, *Burwell vs. Hobby Lobby* was our Supreme Court case about the federal government's mandate that private companies must provide for potentially life-terminating drugs against our religious convictions or pay severe fines. In our case, those fines would have amounted to $1.3 million per day. We knew we could lose the company. What do you do when you fear that you might lose your company?

In the course of our forty-year history, we've had one only other instance when we thought we might lose Hobby Lobby. In that case, we called a family meeting. In those days, we had only my wife, our three children, and their spouses.

We called a family meeting again. But this time, the meeting involved a lot more people—my wife, our children and their spouses, and our grandchildren and their spouses. There were a lot more people involved, and a lot more people depending on us, including thirty-two thousand employees.

It was a big weight. I felt that everyone in the family deserved a say in our course of direction because it affected all of us and the employees we served.

The pressure from the outside world was real. Some folks created Facebook pages opposing us. We struggled sometimes with those who didn't tell the entire story—the care we had for our employees, the drugs we were willing to provide under our health plan, and our long history of providing great wages. We got stacks and stacks of mail—some against us quite bitterly and some for us. It was those who told us that they were praying for us who were such a great comfort.

But the outcome of the case was very much in doubt, and in the months and months of waiting, we put up a billboard outside our office for all to see with a passage from the book of Daniel: "Our God whom we serve is able to deliver us."[1]

Let me say that this is not a book about that Supreme Court case. The seeds for this book were planted long ago, and I'd been working on a draft of this book before the case ever came up. The case only served as a magnifying glass on the issues I want to talk about, like what wealth is, how you can give it away, and how you can build a legacy for your family, in light of all we face today.

For a long time, I've been troubled by what I see in our country. I'm concerned that we've lost something that has made us great. It's big ideas like:

- An invisible legacy was given to us by people who've gone before us.
- Wealth is more than money.
- Wealth is found in our families.
- Part of our legacy is the joy of giving.

These ideas take work and planning. I believe we are living in one of the greatest times in the history of the world. We live in a time of great resources and great need, and thus the greatest good can be accomplished.

But we have to think differently. Will we pass on values and not just valuables? Will we pass on a strong sense of vision and mission for our families? Can we teach our children that giving to God's causes is really, in his eyes, the key to success, both large and small?

Perhaps in a very real sense, how we answer these questions is how we'll "vote" for our lives and for future generations. In the following pages, you'll learn about my own journey in answering these questions—my roots, the struggles I've had in work life, and the questions of what to do with my life and my possessions. I hope that my journey can serve as a guide for your own as you chart your path.

Chapter 2

SHARED VISION

A legacy is created only when a person puts his organization into the position to do great things** without **him.

—John C. Maxwell, Author

I love British cricketer and missionary C. T. Stud's poem "Only One Life." The one line that really gets me is "Only what's done for Christ will last." I have committed myself fully to this. I believe that God has placed us on this earth to work, to earn, and to care for those he has entrusted to us. Yet I also believe that we are put on this earth to give, to devote ourselves to a radical brand of generosity that changes lives and leaves a legacy. To paraphrase God's words to patriarch Abraham, we are blessed so that we can be a blessing.

But what do we mean when we talk about being blessed? In our culture, this might be interpreted as financial blessing. And certainly finances can be part of it. I believe, however, that the blessing God talks about encompasses so much more. Since I have been exceptionally blessed in my life, I have determined to give exceptionally as well. And what about the other ways in which I've been blessed?

Family.

Friends.

Talents.

Freedom.

Education.

I could go on. I'm sure you could too.

When I consider all of the blessings I've been given, it's hard for me not to pause and thank my Lord and my God. His heart is generous. His blessings are wide and rich.

People may know my name now, but I started out like any Joe. Humble beginnings, working hard. But, as God would have it, my story took a turn. It was a turn marked by a faith that pushed me to my limits. Through it all, I learned to trust, and that trust led me onto a path of generosity. I look forward to telling some of the story of this journey in the pages of this book.

My second purpose is to offer the lessons my wife, Barbara, and I learned while trying to fashion a legacy for those who come after us in our family.

And there it is: legacy. What is a legacy, anyway?

The dictionary gives two definitions. First, a legacy is an amount of money or property passed to someone in a will. Second, a legacy is a thing handed down by a predecessor. I want to use the second definition because I believe it includes everything—from belief to right action to finances. You and I possess so much to hand to our predecessors, things seen and unseen.

My story begins in the unseen things. God took me on a wild trip that landed me where I am today, in the land of seen things—my company, Hobby Lobby. But God has taught me that with great wealth and power comes great obligation to the next generation. Knowing this, I have worked through my legacy plan more than once and have finally landed here, writing you my thoughts on the matter.

This is the story I want to recount now. My hope is that others can learn from it and that perhaps our generation can begin doing what few generations before us have done well: pass a true legacy on to those who follow us.

A Modest Plan

I am still sometimes amazed that I have any story worth telling at all. Apart from the grace of God, I might well be entering old age now without any record of success to mention and without any wealth to pass on to my children and grandchildren. Truly, God has been good to me. I think often of the words in Proverbs 19:21: "Many are the plans of a person's heart, but it is the Lord's purpose that prevails."

When I started out in life, I had a few modest plans. I can tell you exactly what they were. First, I wanted to be successful in business. Second, I wanted to have a great marriage. Third, I wanted to raise children who would serve God.

Now these are indeed noble goals and they really were all I wanted when I started out. I had no greater dreams. I remember how dearly I clung to these hopes and how very much they meant to me then. Yet, as aflame as my heart was, I can also imagine how unimpressive I must have seemed to those looking on at the time.

A Counter-Culture Garage Generation

I launched out into the world as a skinny nineteen-year-old just out of the Air Force Reserves. I had no college degree and had done nothing to distinguish myself. I lived in the easy-to-miss red-clay town of Altus, Oklahoma, and I worked at a five-and-dime store called McClellan's. I thought I had everything, particularly since I was newly married to the beautiful and brilliant Barbara Turner. The year was 1961.

Even years later when Barbara and I decided to start a little venture of our own, I still had no dreams beyond the three I started with. That was in 1970. We had determined to launch out into the arts and crafts business by cutting picture frames in our tiny garage.

Thankfully, God had purposes of his own, and they prevailed over my meager plans. That little garage venture later became known as Hobby Lobby. It would have its challenges, and we would make our mistakes. Yet today Hobby Lobby is a company with more than seven hundred stores and nearly thirty thousand employees. By some estimates, it is worth billions of dollars. This blows my mind! This success has allowed us to give hundreds of millions of dollars to God's work around the world and to touch more lives than we had ever dreamed.

It is all God's doing! Barbara and I know this and say it out loud nearly every day of our lives.

But what returns us to the purpose of this book is that the Hobby Lobby story of business success parallels a larger story: the astonishing rise of the baby boomer generation in America.

This eighty-million-strong tribe surprised everyone by moving beyond their hippie, counter-culture beginnings to establishing themselves as one of the most entrepreneurial generations in history. Their creativity, genius, and drive have produced immense fortunes while blessing the world with gifts as stunning as the personal computer and private space travel. Names like Warren Buffet, Steve Jobs, Bill Gates, and a thousand more have become symbols of the inventive, wealth-producing ways of this innovative generation. They have given us decades of entrepreneurial achievements that are often described by commentators simply as miraculous.

A Transfer of Blessings

Like me, though, the baby boomers are now reaching old age. They are in a season both professionally and personally when they are handing off their values, wealth, and control to a younger generation. They are starting to think about legacy, about the imprint of their lives upon their children and their children's children.

Yet it is right here, in the transfer of blessings from one generation to another, that disasters frequently occur. Very often in history, what one generation has created and intended for its heirs fails to embed in the next generation.

Disappointments set in.

Tensions arise.

Purposes are thwarted.

Often, wealth is squandered.

These catastrophes do not necessarily occur because the younger generation is of inferior character or intelligence. Rather, catastrophes occur because the handoff from one generation to the next was never carefully planned, never prepared for over many years so that good would come of it.

It's like a relay race. Perhaps you've seen these races in the Olympics or in a competition between schools in your hometown. Each runner strives to play her role and advance the team. But failures occur, usually at the handoff, the most dangerous moment of the race.

The baton exchange looks simple but demands preparation, timing, and precision. At full speed, one runner must hand off a baton to another runner. You might recall the 2008 Beijing Olympics when the US men's 4 x 100 relay team botched the baton exchange. Four years earlier, in Athens, both the US men's and women's teams botched the handoff, resulting in the women's team being disqualified and the men's team giving Britain the opportunity to pull off the upset, which they did.

The exchange presents countless opportunities for mistakes. The race can, oftentimes, be won or lost at the handoff. Imagine, a small cylindrical baton causing so much chaos. But runners respect the baton. Some might even fear it; they fear the pinging sound it makes when it drops during the exchange, signaling almost instant failure. The coach of the 2012 US relay team in London, Jon Drummond, compared the exchange to two vehicles moving at drastically different speeds on a highway. If you're not precise, if you're not careful, the cars will wreck.

So it is in the lives of generations. We can allow ourselves to get so caught up in running the race of life, of gaining success, of amassing wealth, that we forget that, just around the bend, we have to pass the baton off to the next runner. We forget that other runners await the exchange. And, too often, defeat comes in the handoff.

On the financial side of things, the statistics bear this out. Astonishingly, more than seventy percent of all intergenerational wealth transfers fail.[2] Take the example of family businesses being passed down through family lines. The cold reality is that only about thirty percent of family businesses survive into the next generation, only twelve percent are still viable by the third generation, and only an appallingly small three percent survive into the fourth generation.

On the values side of things, studies suggest that even though the boomer generation drove innovation, job creation, and political success for so long, they also left a bit of an immoral wake. Great wealth and power can, when not managed well, lead to corruption. Boom can lead to bust, unless we're aware of the situation and make a plan to succeed in legacy leaving.

Realities like these haunted Barbara and me as we watched our company succeed. We realized we'd have a valuable monetary legacy to pass on to our children and grandchildren. We prepared in the same way that most parents do—with wills and trusts and the usual instruments of wealth transfer. Yet over time I became uncomfortable with our plan. I could see the potential for loss—to the souls of my children and grandchildren, to our family wealth, and, just as important, to our God-given family mission. We realized that if we mismanaged the seen part of our legacy—the money—we would risk the unseen and invisible aspects of legacy.

That's when I decided to make a change.

End of the Fly Zone

In a relay, the leadoff runner carries the baton in his or her right hand. When the leadoff runner approaches the second leg, he or she must pass the baton, handing it to the next runner's left hand. The second leg runner has a ten meter "fly zone" in which to begin sprinting. This is where the transition begins. But it is in the next twenty meters, an area known as the "passing zone," where the baton exchange occurs.

The passing zone represents the ultimate picture of teamwork. Individual runners, who've spent the last four years preparing for their individual sport as well as beating athletes on their own team, must lay aside their adversarial mentality and cooperate.

They must think of the other runners on their team.

They must approach the race seeking to serve their teammates.

They must run their leg of the race with intensity and passion.

They must not neglect the precision needed for a flawless exchange.

I feel like I am rounding the bend, approaching the handoff point. I'm aiming at the next runner's left hand and planning the handoff.

The other runner has already started sprinting, and here we are, in the fly zone—they're taking off, and I am nearly finished with my part of the race.

Soon, we'll be in the passing zone. Perhaps some of us are there already! When that time comes, I want the transition to be a time of joy as we all contribute to this grand race of life.

This is not just an important time for my generation. It's an important time for the younger generation to prepare for this legacy transfer and begin thinking about their own legacy. It's never too early, and the time is now.

I do not have all the answers, but I do understand how transferring wealth calls upon everything you are, everything you believe, everything you dream for your descendants. It also calls for every ounce of courage you can summon. This is why I hope to help our generation learn the skills of the baton transfer, particularly at this critical time in human history when so much wealth is being transferred and so much opportunity is at hand.

How We're Measured

I opened this chapter with a quote from leadership expert John C. Maxwell. John closes his now indispensable book *The Twenty-one Irrefutable Laws of Leadership* with a chapter titled "The Law of Legacy." He makes the point that only a few leaders learn this law. I would say that's true of most people, not only leaders. Why is that?

He suggests it's because most people achieve on their own. "Achievement comes to someone when he is able to do great things for himself. Success comes when he develops leaders to do great things *for* him. But a legacy is created only when a person puts his organization into the position to do great things *without* him."

"Great, David, but I'm not a leader of an organization. How does this apply to me?"

Well, I'm glad you asked.

My hope and prayer for this book is that it ignites a movement of people who understand their place in history and are excited to make this place better for future generations. In that sense, we are all leaders, we are all contributors to the good of our culture. A teacher or carpenter or pastor or NASCAR driver or ballerina leads in their environment. In our homes and in our parishes, we all lead in some way.

Leaving a legacy is about succession—those who follow after us. John closes the chapter with a great thought to leaders. I want to give it to you here, but I'm going to personalize it for you and me.

"When all is said and done, your ability as a leader will not be judged by what you achieved personally... You will be judged by how well *the generation behind you* did after you were gone. Your lasting value will be measured by succession."[3]

It's hard to measure something you can't see, but that's exactly what I want to do. Those who succeed us will rise not because we are rich beyond all measure but because we pass along the qualities that make us all better human beings.

In the following chapters we'll look at the ideas of an invisible legacy, the joy of and practical how-to's of generosity, the passing of the baton, and the power of the Lord's peace. We'll also look at what it means for a company to be owned by God, and what it means to be rich in God's economy.

Chapter 3

THE INVISIBLE LEGACY

Our days are numbered. One of the primary goals in our lives should be to prepare for our last day. The legacy we leave is not just in our possessions, but in the quality of our lives. What preparations should we be making now? The greatest waste in all of our earth, which cannot be recycled or reclaimed, is our waste of the time that God has given us each day.

—Bill Graham, Evangelist

Do you remember doilies? They were crocheted mats that people might use for decoration on a table or a sofa. On top of taking care of a big family and a big garden, and being a pastor's wife, my mother used to crochet doilies and sell them. Why? Even though my parents gave money together for missions, my mother wanted to make her own offering for missions. So she sold doilies. That memory still sticks with me, and I can say that everything that I have and all that I long to pass on to my descendants has grown from the riches Walter and Marie Green embedded in my life.

In this sense alone, I can say that I was born into a wealthy family.

A legacy of true value is a legacy made of more than money. It's a legacy conceived in wisdom, nurtured by principle, and sustained by character. If we pass only money to the next generation, we lay a crushing load upon them. The inheritance of greater value is the sum of how we live, what we believe, and the content of the dreams that carry us to success. This is what the next generation needs most from us, and what that next generation must prepare to hand off as well.

Fierce Faith

It has often brought a smile to my face to think that if Hobby Lobby had existed during the years I was growing up, my mother might never have darkened the door of one of our stores. Her attention was fixed on beautiful things of another kind, like our family, and her spending was limited by the challenging life she and my father chose to live.

My childhood was shaped by my father's work as a pastor in rural churches across Arizona, New Mexico, Texas, and Oklahoma. In a practice that was common among religious denominations at that time, Dad was assigned to a new church about every two years. For me, this meant eight different schools by the time I finished high school. None of these churches ever seemed to grow much larger than a hundred souls. As a result, small towns, small churches, and small incomes defined our lives, making it a constant challenge for my parents to care for our family of eight.

We usually lived in a two-bedroom house. With five siblings, that meant my brother and I often made do with a rollaway bed in the kitchen. We never had a car. Our parents assured us that we each had two good feet to get us where we needed to be. Generous cousins frequently sent secondhand clothes, so my parents had to provide only underwear and socks for us. The people in our churches supplemented our meager income with weekly "poundings."

Poundings were times during our church services when the faithful brought vegetables, fruit, and other food—often by the pound, hence the name—to the altar to help fill their pastor's pantry that week. Even with this generosity, we often went weeks without seeing meat on the table. Believe me, I learned early the difference between wants and needs.

I don't say any of this to complain. I'm grateful for the life my family lived when I was a boy. I am the son of two people whose feet were firmly planted in this world and yet who kept their eyes and hearts fixed on the world to come. A deep and unshakable faith in Jesus Christ flowed from my parents and filled our home. It was in their lifeblood. Mom and Dad actually met at the same tent meeting where my father went to the altar to receive salvation—and my grandfather and my mother were the ones preaching at the time!

What I learned from the fierce faith of my parents has shaped every day of my life since. I can still remember hearing their voices raised in prayer and how they cried out to God for their children and for the lost people of our various communities. The sound of their singing still plays in my mind and moves me deeply. They trusted in Jesus Christ completely, and because they did, we saw an almost unceasing stream of miracles. My faith grew as I saw God faithfully provide for our needs again and again.

Yet my parents were the kind of people who added to their faith a deep desire to live out the character of Jesus. They were so scrupulous that they refused to tell their children there was a Santa Claus. It wasn't true, so it didn't need to be said. They also never flattered someone just to gain an advantage over them. They were quite willing, though, to offer a genuine compliment along with the words of encouragement and faith that seemed constantly on their lips.

Our family was in church three times a week without fail—not just because our dad was the preacher but because we were focused on pleasing God in all things. When the high school happened to schedule my older sister's graduation ceremony on a church night, it led to a serious conversation in our house about whether we would even attend. In the end, we showed up at the graduation, but this was a rare exception. Following God and being in his house on a regular basis was a core value for us.

Poor but Generous

As surprising as it may sound, my parents were also some of the most generous people I've ever known. This may not seem to fit the picture I've painted of their spare living and meager income, but it was true. I had seen evidence of my parents' generosity through the years in a thousand different ways. Mother might have only three or four dresses in her closet, but if she heard of a woman who needed one, you could be sure Mother would soon arrive at the woman's doorstep with a dress in hand. Such acts were repeated time and again.

Yet the most stunning evidence I ever saw of my parents' generosity came late in the 1960s. My younger brother, James, offered to help my father put his financial books in order. Working through records from many years, James concluded that the most my father ever made in a week was a paltry $138.

We weren't that surprised when we heard this. We always knew our parents received little money in return for their labors. What astonished us, though, were the many canceled checks written to churches for as much as $100. We soon realized that our parents often gave almost their entire weekly salary back to the churches they served. What amazing generosity! What big souls!

Mama Babe Teaching Eternity

More than anyone else, my mother taught me the difference between what is temporal and what is eternal. It says in James 4:14, "What is your life? You are a mist that appears for a little while and then vanishes."

I take nothing away from my father by saying that my mother was the primary influence in my life. There is no question my father was a fine man. He labored for the Lord with all he had. The strain of his ministry sometimes took its toll. This was not something he would have allowed to burden his children. He was from an English background and was a reserved, proper man. He was not expressive or openly affectionate. He kept most of what he felt to himself, confiding only in his wife.

In later years, when I saw him playing joyously with his grandchildren, it pleased me that he could finally give himself to emotions that he had held in check all during his early life.

The simple truth is that my mother was an exceptional woman. I can still picture her so clearly. She was a natural beauty with red hair and fair skin, the kind of woman who needed no makeup to draw attention to herself. She was born just after the turn of the century and raised in the Pentecostal tradition. So she always wore dresses that covered her knees and revealed little of her neck and arms. Her beauty was there anyway.

She was from a German heritage and radiated the great warmth often displayed by her people. Some who met her for a few moments on the street would remember her smile all their days. That smile seemed to draw its brilliance from the joy she found in Jesus. People commented often about this joy and about the burning passion she had to see the gospel spread in whatever small community we were in at the time and in all the nations of the world.

Mother understood that life in this world is short and that only what is done for God will last. Her unswerving emphasis on this truth is probably the reason that all of my brothers and sisters eventually went into some form of full-time ministry.

I don't think my brothers and sisters will be offended if I say that I was Mother's favorite. I was able to make her laugh no matter what else was going on, and the child who can make their mother laugh is usually the favorite. I used to call her Mama Babe, and this would always draw a chuckle from her.

Yet my brothers and sisters will also agree that I was the black sheep of the family. In a family of ministers, I was the only one who did not become a preacher or an evangelist. I think this worried my mother. In fact, I know it did, and the reason I know is that though she never saw what would become of my life, the little bits of early success she did know about made her wonder whether I was really serving the Lord.

Finding Beauty in Retail?

I imagine my parents also worried because I never did well in school. I had to repeat the seventh grade, and I barely got out of high school. I sometimes tell people that school was my worst subject! Of course, attending eight different schools didn't help.

The problem wasn't that I couldn't think or reason. I did love to read, and I devoured books about famous men, about their challenges and how they achieved success. I drank in tales of heroes like Daniel Boone and Abraham Lincoln. Yet I read these books largely on my own. What was happening in the classroom held almost no fascination for me, and this is why I did so poorly.

One of the best things my teachers ever did for me was to put me in a program of "distributive education." Today this would be called "work study." Whatever the name, the idea that I could get school credit for working a part-time job seemed like a miracle to me at the time. This is what landed me at McClellan's, the five-and-dime store in Altus, Oklahoma, that I mentioned earlier.

It was at this store that I found my calling.

I probably wouldn't have said these words in those days. I'd been taught that people with callings became preachers and missionaries. There was no category in our theology for people who were called to "secular" pursuits, like business. Now, though, I realize that a man can be as called to business as any preacher has ever been called to the ministry. But back in those days, devotion to business proved I was backsliding!

The truth is that I fell in love with retail. I cranked out price stickers, scrubbed toilets spotless, and meticulously arranged our store's display window late at night like a painter laboring over his canvas. There was a beauty in it all to me.

I didn't feel like the business of a store was low or unimportant. I loved the idea of providing what people needed. I found that presenting goods attractively or making a store an inviting place was a thrilling challenge. I know not everyone who works in retail feels this way, but I had found my life's work, and the evidence was the great joy I felt in nearly every task.

Finding My Love in a Store

I not only found a love of business in that store, I also found the love of my life. She was a pretty, young part-timer in the stationery department named Barbara. Neither of us will claim it was love at first sight. In fact, Barbara's first impression of me as a seventeen-year-old stock boy was that I was a little smart-aleck. Thankfully, that opinion gradually changed for the better.

Like me, she had parents whose example prepared her to live a life of service to Jesus Christ. Osie and Ina Turner were not in formal ministry, but they lived in such a way that they touched many lives. They routinely kept itinerant missionaries in their home and gave generously to their church. Osie drove around town on Sunday mornings to pick up migrant workers for a Spanish-language church service, and then he drove them home afterward.

I was making only $60 a week when Barbara and I married. Had she stayed in her job, we would have made $100 a week. We could have used that extra money. Yet we agreed that we wanted a strong marriage and we wanted to raise children committed to Jesus. So we decided that Barbara would not work at the store but stay home to build the family of our dreams.

Ah, Success

By the grace of God, I had success in the retail business from the start. My God-given gifts emerged. I found new ways of doing things. I received promotions, earned pay increases, and enjoyed things my family had never been able to, like a car and a larger house.

As this success came to me, I called my mother to tell her about it. I think she was proud of me, but she was also concerned. Believing as she did that business was a secular pursuit, she worried I was becoming too entangled with the things of this world. Our conversations went something like this.

"Hey, Mom, I'm twenty-one and the youngest store manager!"

"David, that's great. What have you done for the Lord lately?"

"Hey, Mom, I'm now a district manager over all these stores."

"Yes, David, but what are you doing for the Lord?"

I could have told my mother that I'd been elected president of the United States and she would have said the same thing: "What are you doing for the Lord?" She understood and lived by the idea that there was only one thing worth doing in this life and that was serving God.

My mother died before she could see what God eventually did with Hobby Lobby. I think she would have recognized that a business can be used for the good of the kingdom of God and that my work as a businessman was indeed a calling from God.

I regret that she never saw it, but I do not regret that she constantly urged me to do great things for God. All the good that Hobby Lobby has done springs from the legacy my father and mother left me.

Finding My Whatever

Though I have told the story of Hobby Lobby's rise in my book *More Than a Hobby*, I want to tell it briefly here because that story is part of the legacy of faith and values that this, my second book, is all about.

It all started in our garage. The year was 1970. By that time, I had left McClellan's and begun working at another five-and-dime chain called TG&Y, the Walmart of that era. I noticed there was a growing market for miniature picture frames, and I thought I saw an opportunity to launch a venture of our own.

Along with my friend and partner, Larry Picco, I went to a bank hoping to borrow $600 in order to buy a frame chopper and the materials to construct the frames. Thankfully, the bank agreed. That $600 was the seed that eventually grew into Hobby Lobby.

We cut the forms out in our garage and then brought them inside to glue together. What a sight! I sure wish we had a picture of all of us—Barbara, little Mart and Steve, and me, with little Darsee nearby—working together around the kitchen table.

I was still working full time at TG&Y at the time, so Barbara and the boys made more frames than I did. We paid the little guys seven cents per frame. Making these frames is how they earned their bubble gum money.

A traveling salesman took our first samples and found buyers and new orders for our "factory." This allowed us to make more frames and to take the baby steps of employing others to help put the frames together. Eventually, we had enough to open our first store in 1972.

The first Hobby Lobby was three hundred square feet, and we had just about $3,000 worth of beads, sequins, a few art supplies, and our miniature frames. That's it. Many days, only one or two customers came through the door.

Yet, slowly, steadily, we prospered.

A year later we moved into an old house that was a thousand square feet. Hippies came into the store and sat down on the carpet to string together beads.

In 1975, we opened our second store and I left TG&Y to go full time with our growing business. At fifty-five thousand square feet, the old shopping center where we opened our second store seemed almost ridiculously huge. We started out using only six thousand feet of the space and gradually grew our way into the rest of it. We had success, I believe, because we focused on keeping things simple and providing a good selection.

During this time, a verse from the book of Ecclesiastes was often on my mind: "Whatever your hand finds to do, do it with all your might."

For me that whatever was providing people with craft and home decor supplies. It was certainly not glamorous, but from the beginning, we focused on doing the little things well while serving and representing the Lord. Over time, we saw God's blessing on our efforts.

Seeing the Invisible

When I recount these stories, I get nostalgic. But there's more to remembering our pasts than warm fuzzy memories. It allows us to see how God carried us. In the moment, we don't always see. But looking back gives us a great view of his provision. A little reflection reveals the values my parents passed on to me.

I can see how my legacy began with my parents' example of fierce faith and contentment. They knew what God wanted them to do, and they did it with everything they had.

I learned from their radical generosity. They gave from nothing. It's one thing to give from full coffers, quite another to give back to God what he's given to you monetarily. Their generosity is etched into my heart.

My mother gave me a heavenly perspective. She was my equalizer. She gave me eyes to see the difference between what carries temporal significance and what carries eternal worth. I might have shrugged and hem-hawed while learning it, but looking back I now see how my mom taught me discernment.

From my early days of retail work, I learned to pay attention to that feeling of contentment when my hands found something they loved doing. A calling can be anything from retail work to landscaping to carpentry to homemaking. We're each wired differently and have something unique and significant to contribute.

My marriage teaches me daily. I can see how making a commitment to our marriage and sticking to our decision for our family structure created peace, stability, and grace.

The legacies our generation hopes to pass on to the next generation are not made of money alone. Money is important, and we should be grateful we have enough to give to our children. Yet the greater part of our legacies is made of invisible things.

They are the family stories we have to recount.

They are the values those stories have to teach.

They are the dreams and the labors and the times of God's provision that have made something of value, not only material wealth but the values that are greater than money.

Invisible qualities, not money, make life worth living. Because of these qualities, we can build a legacy worth passing on. But sometimes we will need to lean on these qualities when no relief is in sight. Like we did when we faced the government in its own court.

Part 2

IT'S ALL GOD'S

For it is in giving that we receive.

—St. Francis

There is not a square inch in the whole domain of our human existence over which Christ, who is Sovereign over all, does not cry, Mine!

—Abraham Kuyper

Everything was created through him;
nothing—not one thing!—
came into being without him.
What came into existence was Life,
and the Life was Light to live by.
The Life-Light blazed out of the darkness;
the darkness couldn't put it out.

—John the Beloved

Chapter 4

THE RULE OF PEACE

Relying on God has to begin all over again every day as if nothing had yet been done.

—C. S. Lewis, Writer

How do you and I get to the point where we can give everything away? Before we can give in such a way, we need to realize who owns everything in the first place. I always believed that everything I owned was God's, until reality tested me.

This is the story in which I learned the wonderful riches of peace. And not just any peace but the kind that passes all understanding. All that I've said so far about generosity and legacy can happen only when we have the peace that recognizes everything is God's.

As it turns out, this crazy kind of heavenly peace requires that you, or in this case I, be willing to give everything up. No guarantees. No safety net. Getting it all back again is not part of the equation. Only the willingness to lay it all on the line. In this story, the all was my entire company.

So You Want to Sue the US Government?

In September 2012, I found myself suing the government of the United States. Loyal, patriotic American that I am, this came as quite a shock to me. It still surprises me when I think back on it today.

The reason for this lawsuit is now pretty widely known. On March 23, 2010, President Barack Obama signed into law The Patient Protection and Affordable Care Act, better known as the Affordable Care Act or, simply, Obamacare. It was a massive and controversial overhaul of America's healthcare system. Its stated goal was to "increase the number of Americans covered by health insurance and decrease the cost of health care."[4]

As benevolent as that may sound, the reality was that the act placed huge burdens upon American citizens and corporations. For the first time in the history of our country, every US citizen would be required to have health insurance. Health providers were informed they would eventually have to cover the cost of a wide variety of preventive care. The law even set limits on the profits that insurance companies could earn.

What brought my family and our company into conflict with this law were some specifics about the kind of care private companies were required to provide for their employees.

We were certainly not opposed to caring generously for our workers. For years Hobby Lobby had paid wages far above the industry standard and had paid a self-imposed minimum wage several times the federal requirement. We closed on Sundays so that workers could be with their families and closed early on weekdays for the same reason. Our insured workers enjoy the services of a free onsite medical clinic, the care of company chaplains, the opportunities of educational programs, and many other generous benefits. None of this came about as a result of external pressure. We offered these benefits because we believe that a Christian company should take good care of its employees.

In short, we weren't opposed to providing insurance or any other reasonable benefits for our workers. Our problem with the requirements of the Affordable Care Act was their insistence that we pay for medications that terminate pregnancies after conception. This meant that we were being required to pay for abortions, a practice that we as biblical Christians believe is counter to God's will.

As I wrote in an article for *USA Today* on the day we filed our lawsuit, "Being Christians, we don't pay for drugs that might cause abortions. Which means that we don't cover emergency contraception, the morning-after pill or the week-after pill. We believe doing so might end a life after the moment of conception, something that is contrary to our most important beliefs."[5]

What was as disturbing as the abortion requirements of the healthcare law was the fact that the government was allowing exceptions to the law for a wide variety of reasons but refused to do so for religious reasons. This was un-American. We believed it was un-Constitutional. We also knew that it was a violation of the Religious Freedom Restoration Act, signed into law by President Bill Clinton in 1993, which had guaranteed that the "government shall not substantially burden a person's exercise of religion even if the burden results from a rule of general applicability."

Not only was the federal government creating a "burden" on our free exercise of religion, but it was also threatening to fine us $1.3 million a day if we did not comply with its unjust and immoral law. I was as furious as any patriot could be at mistreatment by my own government. As I wrote in that same *USA Today* article, "Our government threatens to fine job creators in a bad economy. Our government threatens to fine a company that's raised wages four years running.

Our government threatens to fine a family for running its business according to its beliefs. It's not right."

As determined as we were on the day we filed this now famous lawsuit, there had been a great deal of discussion and soul-searching beforehand. I don't mind admitting that I was fearful during this time. I lost a lot of sleep. I imagined we would lose the company if things went badly, and I felt the pressure of it every day.

Yet I also felt the weight of the evil that was being forced upon us. The idea that my government would force me to pay for the killing of the unborn seemed to me an abomination, and it was an abomination that had been creeping through our land for at least a generation. I reflected on this often while I tried to decide how we should respond to this unjust law.

My Faith Challenged

I was born in 1941. This means that I came into the world right at the leading edge of the baby boomers, most of whom were born just after their soldier fathers and mothers began returning from World War II in 1945. One of the events that defined our generation happened in 1947, well before we were old enough to understand its importance.

In that year, the US Supreme Court ruled in a case called *Everson v. Board of Education* that "the First Amendment has erected a wall between church and state. That wall must be kept high and impregnable." The practical result of these words was that religion and the American government had to be kept completely separate. It was a horrible ruling that tortured the intent of the First Amendment and gave it meaning none of the founding fathers intended.

Yet it was on the basis of this disastrous ruling that my generation was forced to endure the dismantling of religious rights that had been carefully preserved by generations of our ancestors. We saw prayer taken out of the public schools in 1962 and the Ten Commandments taken off the walls of our schools and civic buildings soon after. We saw students forbidden to pray on their own time on school grounds in 1970, and this followed students being forbidden even to pray aloud over their own school lunches in 1965.

Bibles, religious instruction, prayers at graduations, prayers at football games, and even the mention of Jesus Christ in state legislatures were all banned by some court somewhere in America, and all in fear that the "separation of church and state"—words that don't even appear in our Constitution—would be violated.

With this attempt to eradicate religion in American public life came a horrible moral slide in our culture. Nothing represented this more darkly to me than the Supreme Court's 1973 *Roe v. Wade* ruling. Rather than let states decide the matter of abortion for themselves, the Supreme Court issued an unscientific, un-Constitutional, and un-American ruling that made abortion legal nationwide. Since that day, according to National Right to Life, more than fifty-seven million abortions have occurred in the United States.[6]

It is important to understand that, for Christians like me, each of these abortions is the taking of a human life. I believe, and millions of Americans believe, that once conception has taken place in the body of a mother, a new human being exists. We don't believe that a fetus becomes a person many months into a pregnancy. Nor do we believe, as some do, that a fetus isn't a child until it is born. No, we believe that upon conception, a new life exists, a life that must be protected, cherished, and brought lovingly into the world. We believe this child has rights from the moment it is conceived.

It shouldn't be hard to understand, then, that when the US government ordered the company I had started and built on Christian principles to pay for the killing of human beings in the womb, I just couldn't do it. I had to file a lawsuit to stop this challenge to our beliefs. I was also grieved that it had ever come to this in the United States of America.

Lions, Lambs, and Monkeys

Fortunately, I wasn't alone, and by this I mean that I had my family around me to give me counsel and to stand with me.

The Lord has blessed Barbara and me with three unique children. The oldest is Mart, the son Barbara likes to call "our lion." Typical of first-born children, Mart possessed the gifts of a natural leader from an early age. He has a strong personality, a healthy dose of common sense, and an inner intensity that makes him the kind of man who knows how to get things done. His discipline and focus brought him success in his early academic and sports careers. In later years, these attributes combined with his deep Christian commitment and his leadership strengths to make him a success in ministry and business. His accomplishments are vast, and he is always a source of wise counsel and clear vision for me.

If Mart is our lion, then Steve, our second son, is our lamb. Steve is quieter and more thoughtful than I am. He listens patiently, mulls things over, and speaks purposefully. His leadership style is firm but gentle, the fruit of his innate kindness but also his gift for deep reflection.

I suppose in the manner of most fathers, I wanted my sons to be like me, to think like me, and work like me. Steve was far different from me, and, frankly, I found it frustrating. I had decided that I needed to "train" Steve in the ways of business. The truth is I came down on him rather forcefully at times. One day I was praying about this challenge and the Lord seemed to impress me with this thought: "You're not training him, you're trying to change him. What you want Steve to be is not who he is."

I knew immediately that this was true. I went to my son and said, "Steve, I'm sorry. I've been dead wrong in how I've related to you. I need to find out who you really are, and then help you find your place. We're not all the same."

Once I began to work with the way the Lord made Steve and not against it, I had the privilege of seeing him spread his wings and become an amazing leader. Today, he is the president of our company. He's perfect for this role, and I'm thankful every day for the unique being God made him to be.

The third of our three children is Darsee. If Mart is our lion and Steve is our lamb, Darsee is our monkey! Barbara says often that "to know Darsee is to love her." She is vivacious, creative, and a fount of happiness. Her energy and passion are contagious. Someone once said that Darsee doesn't throw parties, she is the party! She's also one of the most considerate people I know. I carry a little notebook with me to jot down notes and reminders—pecking away on a smart phone isn't for me!—and often I open it up to find a note of encouragement in the swirling handwriting I know can only have come from Darsee.

I'm pleased that each of my children has married well. Mart's wife, Diana, has been a constant source of support for him in all of his many endeavors, and she loves being a mother to her children and grandchildren. Steve's wife, Jackie, is involved in so many ways, including the ministry work of Museum of the Bible. Darsee married Stan, who is engaged in the business of Hobby Lobby.

We Must Be Together

A family like the one I've described becomes even dearer in times of crisis. And this is why I turned to them when the government started making the excessive demands of the new healthcare law on our company.

I knew that the law put our company in danger.

I knew we could pay $1.3 million a day in fines for only so long before going bankrupt.

I also knew that whatever we did, if the company survived, my heirs would live in the wake of this decision all their lives.

I could not act alone. I had to seek their counsel and hope for agreement in whatever we chose to do.

Now, I am not the sort of man who thinks a family company can be run by bringing the whole crew together for every decision. This was one of the rare times I did it, and it was because the decisions I made in this crisis had the potential to affect us all in huge ways. This was about much more than decorative designs for new fabric or where to open the next store. We were in a fight for the very existence of the business and for the values we all held dear. We had to be together.

I asked Mart to call a meeting. As he did, I was immensely grateful for the time we had all spent in previous years hammering out our values, our mission, the principles of our faith, and our philosophy of inheritance. Those hours of discussion—the crafting of language, the working for agreement on beliefs and goals, and, ultimately, the embracing of a plan for the use of wealth—had brought us together and solidified us in a way I had never dreamed.

We were strong, unified, filled with common vision, and eager for the future, and all just as we were forced to face a dire crisis. I did not know exactly what was going to happen, but I did know that God had worked so marvelously in our family that we could endure anything.

Now, in our family and company, we use the shorthand G2 and G3 for Generation 2 and Generation 3. The G2 refers to our children, our second generation. The G3 refers to our third generation, our grandchildren. There are always G4s running around somewhere. But this meeting was Barbara and me with the G2 and G3 of our family.

I recall having a bit of concern as I approached the meeting. Though I was fairly confident that everyone in our family felt about abortion as Barbara and I did, I also knew that the millennials in our world approach the issue of abortion differently from their parents and grandparents. Even if they feel the same about when life begins in the womb, they can often have very different perspectives on how society should handle abortion and about whether the Christian church should even address the issue publicly.

As much confidence as I had in the faith of my grandchildren—my G3s—I still wasn't sure what their counsel would be. Though the decision ultimately was Barbara's and mine, I deeply wanted agreement and support from my entire family.

The Big Meeting

In September 2012, we all gathered at Mart's home. I carefully laid out the challenges before us. The mood was somber, thoughtful, but no one panicked and fear didn't rule us.

After everything was explained, Steve spoke up. I was never so grateful for his deep maturity and his many years of devouring and meditating upon the scriptures. Steve looked around the room and then thoughtfully began to recount the Old Testament story of Daniel and his three Hebrew friends.

Steve said that there were three ways our crisis could unfold, and each of them was found in Daniel's story. In one episode, Daniel was required to eat meat that was unclean according to Jewish law. Steve said that in this case, Daniel and his friends appealed for a change in diet and it was granted. This might happen for us, he said. We might seek relief and receive favor.

However, a second option might be that things go against us and that we find ourselves "in the lion's den," just as Daniel found himself in a real lion's den. Deliverance came to him at the very last minute. The same might happen for us. Perhaps God would be most glorified by rescuing us as we were just about to be devoured.

Then Steve quietly reminded us that God uses suffering. It might not be pleasant to think about and it isn't popular in most Christian preaching today, but it is undeniable in the pages of the Bible. We might be required to suffer. It might be the will of God. We should be ready to embrace whatever hardships come as the price of obeying God.

Everyone thought about these words. We knew we had come to a moment of destiny for our family. I think we all felt the same thing. Whatever might come, we wanted to do the will of God. I asked that everyone say whatever he or she had to say. There were some questions, but most who spoke expressed their fierce belief that we had to stand for life, that God had allowed us to be in this situation so we could take just such a stand.

There was some more discussion, and then we took a vote. It was unanimous. We would fight in court against the unjust demands of this new law.

Hearing my children and grandchildren speak with conviction, with a desire to serve and honor God no matter the cost, freed me from my fear. From that time on, I gave the whole situation to God. I realized I was worrying about something that was not mine to carry.

Hobby Lobby is God's. So was that decision and the future of the company.

I told the media, "This is not mine. It's God's, and I am going to lean on him. Whether or not the company survives the outcome of the Supreme Court's decision on our case."

There are times when you simply have to declare your faith for the entire world to see. We did this by putting a huge sign outside of our executive offices in Oklahoma City that read, "Our God whom we serve is able to deliver us."

We rested in that truth.

If God's deliverance included the loss of the company, it would greatly impact our thirty thousand employees. Our family knew this and thought that it was more important that God be glorified than that our family win its case. Even if we lost, it could be a win for God's glory if he used the loss to call people around the nation to prayer and action.

Suing the Government

And so it began.

On September 12, 2012, Hobby Lobby filed suit in the US District Court for the Western District of Oklahoma against the federal mandate forcing us to provide and pay for four potentially life-terminating drugs and devices. Though this federal mandate would not apply to us until January 1, 2013, we knew this lawsuit would not be resolved before then. Therefore, we also asked the district court for an injunction to stop this law from applying to us until such time as the court could rule on the merits of our case.

This was important. Remember, if we did not get this injunctive relief, we would be faced with fines for as much as $1.3 million per day. On November 11, 2012, the district judge denied our request for an injunction. Time was not on our side.

We immediately appealed the district court's decision to the Tenth Circuit Court of Appeals in Denver, Colorado. It did not go well. On December 20, the tenth circuit agreed with the district court that our case did not have a substantial likelihood of success. This meant that the mandate would apply to us on January 1, 2013.

Our lawyers then appealed this tenth circuit order to the US Supreme Court. We filed an Emergency Application for Relief that would be ruled on by the Supreme Court justice who was responsible for matters such as this from the tenth circuit—Justice Sonia Sotomayor. On December 27, 2012, Justice Sotomayor denied our request for relief.

We were heartbroken.

While this did not mean the end of our lawsuit, it did mean that if we did not comply with the mandate while our lawsuit was pending in the court system, which could take years, we would be faced with those massive daily fines.

With only four days to go before the fines kicked in, the one and only option we had left was to go back to the tenth circuit and see if the entire court, all eleven judges at the time, would hear our request for relief. We still had a few legal options, but it was highly doubtful that we would get any help before January 1. Our attorneys even told us that a brief could not be filed and ruled upon before the end of the year. We were out of options, or so I thought.

On Friday, December 28, 2012, our general counsel, Peter Dobelbower, came to my office and told me that he had discovered a way to keep the fines from applying to us until July 1, 2013, thus giving us some much needed breathing room while the tenth circuit decided whether to hear our case *en banc*, which means all of the justices, rather than just a few, forming a panel.

Peter discovered that we could change our "plan year" from a calendar year to a fiscal year, with a July 1 anniversary date. What this meant was that the contraceptive mandate would not apply to us until July 1, 2013. At $1.3 million per day in fines, this change could save us nearly $250 million.[7]

The granting of a hearing before an entire US circuit court of appeals (en banc) is extremely rare. As an example of just how rare this is, not one circuit court in the nation granted an en banc hearing during the many cases that were originally filed challenging the constitutionality of the Affordable Care Act.

We knew we were swimming upstream, but on January 11, 2013, we filed our request for an en banc hearing before the tenth circuit court of appeals. Our brief was supported by eleven different Friend of the Court briefs that included support from US senators and members of Congress, the State of Oklahoma, and other likeminded organizations.

Then, on March 29, the tenth circuit granted our request and set oral arguments for May 23. Finally, we got our first victory and were able to breathe a little easier—for the time being.

On June 27, 2013, four days before we would start being fined $1.3 million per day, the tenth circuit issued a 165-page written order containing six different opinions from eight different tenth circuit judges.

The tenth circuit essentially said that corporations like Hobby Lobby can make a claim under the Religious Freedom Restoration Act, and that the government was prohibited from enforcing the mandate against us.

We knew this wasn't our final victory, but we were still elated. Not long after, the federal government appealed the tenth circuit's decision to the US Supreme Court. We weren't surprised. There were a large number of cases regarding this oppressive law making their way to the Supreme Court. We were at least thankful the matter was about to be decided at the highest level.

Then came a huge surprise.

Headed to the Highest Court

Though the Supreme Court had dozens of cases before it that related to the same matters of law we were appealing, they chose to hear our case. The justices could have chosen to hear any of the other cases. Their ruling on any one of them would have resolved the issues in all the cases. Yet the court chose to hear ours.

This meant that a case called *Burwell v. Hobby Lobby Stores, Inc.* entered the annals of the US Supreme Court and thus the pages of American history.[8] We couldn't help but see this as the hand of God.

A few months later, on March 25, 2014, the Supreme Court heard oral arguments in our case. The principle of law it was considering was whether the government has the power to force a family business to violate their sincerely held religious beliefs. This is a critical issue in our increasingly secular age, and I found myself constantly thanking the Lord that our company was on the forefront of the battle.

What I felt most during the oral arguments of the case surprised even me. I felt a deep, unshakeable, undeniable peace. I sat in that awe-inspiring courtroom with its soaring columns, its busts of great men of the past, and its regal furnishings. And I marveled at the peace that enveloped me.

I knew my company was on the line.

I knew huge matters of faith and justice I cared very much about would be decided in the coming months as a result of this case.

I also knew the world was watching.

None of it shook me, and this was not because I am a rock of conviction or because I'm an unemotional person. This peace was the gift of God and the fruit of the prayerful decisions my family and I had made.

I think of the peace I had at that time much as I think about the peace I have in the face of death. I have entrusted my life to Jesus Christ. I know where I will go after I die. I do not fear death, and I do not worry about it. A decision has been made. I belong to God. That decision resolves all things. I feel nothing but peace about leaving this world.

It was much the same as I sat in that courtroom. My family and

I knew who we were. We had a God-given mission. We had even put that mission down on paper for all of us to affirm. We also knew who the company belonged to. It belonged to God and him alone. Based on this, we had designed some unusual plans for what would happen to the company after we were gone and how the wealth from it would be used.

We had resolved all of this and done so in complete agreement as a family. I'll reveal more about this in the pages to come, but for now let me say that this is what gave me peace that day in the Supreme Court building.

I knew who I was.

I knew who my family was.

I knew who owned Hobby Lobby.

I knew why we were in that courtroom.

I knew who controlled my fate no matter what those justices decided. And peace reigned.

A Monumental Ruling

In June 2014, the court ruled. In a 5-4 vote, the justices decided in favor of Hobby Lobby. It was a huge victory. I imagine that during the days preceding the court's ruling we were the most prayed for family in the world. It all paid off. God granted not just the Green family but also the cause of justice and righteousness a great victory. We were thankful beyond words.

Yet what I'm eager to emphasize is that at a great juncture in my family's story, peace ruled because we had already done some difficult homework. These decisions made the experience of our legal battles not just survivable but survivable in peace.

The same is true for how we have planned to handle the transfer of wealth from one generation to another in our family. The same bedrock decisions establish us and give us peace for that all-important juncture too.

The Seed of Legacy

I'm grateful Hobby Lobby won its great legal battle. I think it was a victory for our country. But there's also a bigger picture here. I gained some wisdom through this experience. It's my hope that I can offer some of it as we discuss the importance of the generational handoff in the pages that follow.

But before we go there, I want to stress the importance of building a foundation of virtues in your life. I gave you a glimpse into my days as a boy and how my parents instilled certain qualities within me. It's the invisible elements of legacy we so often take for granted. But it was those principles taught by my parents early on that formed me into the man I am today.

Your work ethic matters. So does mine.

How you and I treat our spouses matters. It builds into our children, close friends, and relatives.

What we spend our time doing matters. It reveals our heart's desire. Our true treasure.

We don't always think about these characteristics that form our everyday experience, but if I've learned anything from my parents and my experience, it's all that matters.

I hope that the decisions my family made will inspire others to lock down the core values that will define them and the next generation. That will make it possible for them to go through crises in peace and, ultimately, in true prosperity.

Chapter 5

A COMPANY OWNED BY GOD

I love the quaint saying of a dying man, who exclaimed, "I have no fear of going home; I have sent all before me; God's finger is on the latch of my door, and I am ready for Him to enter."

—Charles Haddon Spurgeon,
British Preacher

I have listened to many successful business owners tell their stories through the years, and a surprising truth seems to surface in nearly all of their experiences. It is the truth that the hard times were often when they learned the lessons that took them from good to great. They took the time to "mine the valleys," to learn the lessons the bitter seasons had to teach. Because they did, they rose to greatness on the strength of character and wisdom they never would have had without the benefits of hardship.

My story is very much the same. Without two critical lessons I learned at difficult junctures in my life and business, we wouldn't be where we are today. Nor would we have learned to honor God, who is the owner of it all, as we have.

Father and Provider

The first of these lessons came in the middle of the 1980s. For nearly a decade, the oil industry in our country had been exploding with prosperity. It was boom time, as they say in Texas, and money was flowing freely. It seemed it would never end.

By that time, we had twelve stores. Most of them were in Oklahoma, so we enjoyed the benefits of the free-flowing money that came from the free-flowing petroleum in our state. There was so much money washing through our state's economy that you could sell almost anything, and that is what led to our first major crisis.

We had become successful through the years as a crafts store. It was what we knew and what people wanted us to be. We should have stayed in our sweet spot. Instead, we got off track. The attraction of bigger profits in a strong economy made us veer into realms we should not have attempted to be in. For example, we started selling expensive luggage, grandfather clocks, ceiling fans, and even signed and numbered lithographs for high prices. We didn't stop there. We sold gourmet food for a while and even offered a whole line of miniature brass oil rigs.

Why not? Money flowed like water in those days.

We were off track, though, and had lost our way a bit. We just didn't know it. The free-flowing cash seemed to cover our mistakes, camouflaged the fact that we had strayed from our best.

Then came the oil bust of 1985. The money dried up. By the end of that year, we had lost nearly a million dollars. That was a lot of money in those days. It was the first time we had a red-ink year. Even worse, that year's loss was larger than any two years of profit in the history of our company.

Things got even worse. Our bank threatened to call our note.

Suppliers started cutting us off. I didn't know what to do. I started praying like I never had before. I even found myself crawling into the space under my desk to cry out to God for help. It was as if God was saying to me, "You think you are so big that I'm going to let you have this by yourself."

Finally, I knew I had to give my family the bad news. In April 1986, I gathered everyone into our living room. At the time, our three children, two of our nephews, and our future son-in-law all earned their living through the company. I can still recall the awful feeling in the pit of my stomach as I looked them each in the eye and told them that our company was close to ruin.

"We are in serious trouble," I said. "And I don't know what to do."

After a few reflective moments, Mart spoke up. He was just twenty-four years old, but what he said changed my life and our business forever.

Looking at me with deep love and confidence, he said, "Dad, it's okay. Our faith is not in you—it's in God. If we lose the business, we'll still be okay."

Those words mark a humbling and powerful moment in my life that I will never forget. Up until that time, I had given God credit for Hobby Lobby's success, but I am afraid it was only lip service. I do not think I realized until Mart spoke just how much of my confidence and pride had become wrapped up in the ability of my own hands. It is so easy to claim our trust is in God and to say we "give him the glory" while our hearts are still wrapped up in our hidden obsession with control and success. Yet our hearts are never hidden, not from the one who matters. The scriptures tell us, "All a person's ways seem pure to them, but motives are weighted by the Lord" (Prov. 16:2). We are also told, "The Lord does not look at the things people look at. People look at the outward appearance, but the Lord looks at the heart" (1 Sam. 16:7).

I was humbled and moved by what Mart said, but I had no clue what to do. I went for lunchtime walks in the park across the street from our offices, pleading with the Lord to give me direction. In time, he did. He helped me see that we had to get back to our core business and we had to tighten our belts in every area.

We got busy. We found a different lender, worked out deals with our suppliers, and got back to the business we knew best. By the end of 1986, we were out of the red and earning a profit. We have continued to do so ever since. I give credit for that recovery to the one who is my "refuge and strength, an ever-present help in trouble" (Ps. 46:1). My faith in God as Father and Provider and my awareness of my lack of control grew from that time forward and have never left me.

Our profits rose. Our stores multiplied. God showed himself faithful in every step. By 1987, Hobby Lobby was voted the Oklahoma Small Business of the year. In 1997, Ernst and Young selected me as Entrepreneur of the Year.

I Own It All. Signed, God

A second season of hardship also proved fruitful in my life and business. Indeed, it is not going too far to say that what happened during that dark night of the soul has changed everything about who we were as a company.

By the late 1990s, Hobby Lobby had become immensely successful. God's blessing, trends in arts and crafts, and the skills of our leadership team all meant rapid increases in the number of our stores and huge profits.

It was all good news. It was exactly what we had hoped and prayed for. Yet success came with a certain weight, a sense of concern and a burden that pressed down upon me and became nearly oppressive.

The immense profits we were enjoying had become a source of worry to me. I was grateful for them, but I also knew that wealth has to be handled wisely to keep it from being destructive. I was eager to be wise, and this yearning to do the right thing was keeping me up at night.

One night I was praying about this out in the back yard. All of a sudden, right there under the Oklahoma night sky, something dramatic happened. I sensed God saying to me, "This company belongs to me. Don't you touch it. It's mine."

The force of these words jolted me. I connected them right away with the story in the Bible about the day King David and his people tried to move the ark of the covenant into Jerusalem using a cart. Everything went well until one of the handlers, a man named Uzzah, reached out to steady the ark as it went over a bump in the road. God struck him dead on the spot. Why? The Bible says it was "because of his irreverent act" (2 Sam. 6:7). The whole procession came to a grinding halt. Celebration turned into disaster.

I sensed immediately that my worry about Hobby Lobby was largely because there was too much human effort attempting to steady the ark of the company. I truly believed then, as I believe now, that Hobby Lobby is a company God allowed to be born and to endure. If we kept getting in his way, if we kept relying on human strengths and thinking, what kind of trouble awaited us?

I went back in the house and took out a piece of paper. I wrote the following: "I own Hobby Lobby. Signed, God."

From that moment on, it was crystal clear in my mind that this was not my corporation. I had always believed that in some general sense. I had always given God the glory for what Hobby Lobby had become. Yet now God's ownership of the company had come to me in searing revelation.

While I had always believed Hobby Lobby was God's company, after that night it was as though God had laid personal claim. He was not just leaving it to me to acknowledge his ownership with my words. He was enforcing his ownership in my heart and throughout the company. It was as transforming for me that night as it became for our entire company over time.

Someone might well ask, "Did anything change because God exerted his ownership of the company that night?" Yes. The fact that God owns Hobby Lobby has influenced our decisions about how we run the business in many different ways.

Some of our policies were laid in place from the beginning, and others we have added along the way. Each one is vitally important, and I want to focus on three main areas to illustrate how we try to honor God in what we do: our employees; the way we do business, or our ethics; and how we interact with the government.

Our Employees Matter

I believe most people understand that Hobby Lobby has at least some Christian influence behind the wheel. Perhaps this is because they notice our stores are closed on Sundays or perhaps they hear the Christian music we play in our stores.

What people may not know are the decisions we have made with regard to our employees. The men and women who work hard for us throughout the country every day are not just cogs in a massive mechanism. They are real people with real feelings and lives to take care of beyond the workplace.

Henry Ford was a brilliant American inventor and industrialist. He was the genius who came up with the idea of the assembly line. Yet he had just about zero sensitivity to the human side of his business.

He is reported to have complained once, "Why is it that I always get a whole person when all I really want is a pair of hands?"

The people who make my company and yours run successfully out there in Idaho and South Carolina and Pennsylvania—or at the central warehouse—are far more than just a pair of hands or a strong back. They have families to love, neighbors to befriend, and churches or other community needs to serve. They will care about our business only to the extent that we care about their overall welfare.

Once when I was praying about our business, I sensed the Lord saying to me, "You know, I've put these people in your charge. You're responsible for their well-being." The point was not "How much work can I get out of them?" but rather "How well are they doing under my oversight?"

This is the reason, by the way, that we decided long ago to close our stores at 8:00 p.m. instead of 9:00 p.m. or later. We are open only sixty-six hours per week—9:00 a.m. to 8:00 p.m. for six days a week. Few retailers do that. I knew I was going against the tide of American retail. I knew the last hour of the day was one of the most profitable and that my competitors would definitely stay open to pick up the sales I would miss. Yet I could afford to miss those sales, and I could not get away from the human toll that the normal retail schedule was taking on our employees.

I had worked those long evening hours myself for years. I remember dragging myself home late at night, long after my young kids were already in bed. It wasn't healthy. I decided that if I could give my store managers and floor staff just one more hour to be home with their families, it would reduce family stress and help them live more balanced lives. The people who work at Hobby Lobby, and their families, have value far exceeding the sale of a package of sequins or a few yards of fabric. I've never regretted our decision to close an hour early each night.

Our even more "radical" decision to close on Sundays is another result of this concern for employees. Nearly everyone who interviews me seems to ask me about this, and I say, "Well, we think being open sixty-six hours a week is enough for people to come buy what they need. The idea of a 'day of rest' is centuries old. It is not just a Christian thing. The Jewish faith proclaims the same thing, although on Saturday. Muslims take their day on Friday. Apparently there is a rhythm built into the created order. Work no more than six days, then take one off. This rhythm should not be ignored."

Employees see this as a sign of our genuine concern for their well-being. I have received a multitude of emails and notes from our workers expressing their gratitude for this unconventional policy.

With each of these decisions to care for our employees, we see confirmation of an important principle: take care of your workers and you will benefit.

From the decision to close on Sundays, for example, we have experienced a wonderful return: the quality of retail people who apply to work for a six-days-a-week company. We have been amazed to see how many top-notch, family-oriented, solid, productive managers and other employees want to leave the grind where they are and come work for Hobby Lobby. We never anticipated such a ripple effect!

I tell our store managers, "I want you to run a good, profitable store, but if that takes you seventy hours a week, I truthfully don't want you working for me. I don't want a good store at the expense of your kids or your marriage. What I'm asking of you should be able to be done in a five-day workweek that includes two evenings at the store. That's all. And there are hundreds of our managers across the country proving that. So I know it can be done, if you choose the right team and train them to get the job done."

The other major factor in job satisfaction, besides hours, is obviously money. Of course, everyone at every level of every company across America would like to be making a million dollars a year. That's just human nature. Yet this should not become an excuse for ignoring the real needs of workers.

For a long time, I wanted to raise pay rates but hesitated because of the pressure of corporate debt. At least that was my excuse. I told myself we needed to pay down our loans first. Yet, more recently, we've taken action on this front. In 2009, we raised our base pay for full-time people—those who stock shelves, run cash registers, do picture framing for customers, and so forth—to ten dollars an hour. This was when the federal minimum wage was $7.25 an hour.

The next year, we tacked on another dollar per hour.

The next year, we did it again.

The next year, we did it yet again.

Each of these jumps added approximately $10 million to the payroll. Amazingly, it never showed up on the bottom line. Why? Because we were running more profitable stores. Employees were fighting harder for us than they had in the past. They reported stealing more dutifully, and so shrinkage of inventory went down. Our profits have grown each year since we increased pay so dramatically.

The truth is that it has cost absolutely nothing to give these raises. I have come to believe that I cannot afford low-paid help. I do much better when they do better.

During this period, the average longevity of an employee on the sales floor has doubled, from eighteen months to thirty-six months. That has meant fewer replacements to hire and train, which is a savings all around.

Yet it is the personal stories that thrill me the most. Single moms have said with tears, "I was working two jobs to stay afloat; now I don't have to do that! Thank you so much." One person said, "I was just able to buy the first car in my life with an air conditioner!"

I cannot think of anything I have done in forty years of business—besides giving to various ministries—that has been this exciting. I wish I had figured out a way to do this much earlier. It is just as the book of Proverbs says: "Do not withhold good from those to whom it is due, when it is in your power to act" (3:27).

Naturally, the word has spread widely about these wage adjustments. Newspapers have run stories. Internet posts and tweets have gone viral. The result is that the volume of job applications has increased. We now have a larger pool of job candidates than ever, and this allows us to choose the very best. Again, we see that treating people well only benefits the company and its mission.

Our Ethics Matter

Our relations with business people—bankers, co-investors, competitors, suppliers—have also been affected by our faith-based commitment to integrity. We say we intend to treat them forthrightly and respectfully, to observe the Golden Rule of treating others as we would like to be treated.

Question: Is this only what we intend, or does it actually happen?

It does happen, and I could give dozens of examples. If a supplier short-ships something that Hobby Lobby has ordered, we will, of course, point it out: "We ordered a hundred cases of those Christmas ornaments, but you delivered only ninety-two." However, what happens if they mistakenly delivered 106? I have called owners of companies to say, "Hey, we just got your shipment, but instead of a shortage, there's a 'longage.' You sent us more than what the invoice says." They can hardly believe their ears. "Nobody has ever done this before!" they tell me.

Well, we do, because it is right.

If a supplier's representative makes an appointment to see one of our buyers and present his or her product line, I have instructed our team to be present and on time. It is not respectful for the representative to travel halfway across the state and then be told by the receptionist, "Oh, sorry, Jim's not going to be able to see you today—something came up."

If an agreement to purchase is made, the deal needs to be straightforward and clear: a given product for a given price (hopefully, a very good price!) by a certain date. Keep it simple. Do not go back later with "Oh, by the way" adjustments or requests for favors, additional discounts, and so on. The supplier needs to earn a living too.

Just so everyone was clear, I wrote up a sign that hangs on the walls of our interview rooms:

> NOTICE TO VENDORS
>
> It is Hobby Lobby policy that employees or owners will not receive any gifts of any value from vendors.
>
> Except for rare occasions, employees will not accept dinner engagements, as they will be with their families during the evening.
>
> Hobby Lobby owners and buyers will pay their share of lunches. Any gift received by anyone will be returned to the sender.
>
> Any violation of this policy will jeopardize the relationship between Hobby Lobby Stores, Inc., and the vendor.
>
> We thank you in advance for your cooperation.
>
> David Green, CEO

My point here is that favors and kickbacks are not to be considered. If a vendor has to slide something extra under the table to a buyer, it inevitably drives up the vendor's price on the product, which can only hurt my company. I'm told that one-third of all corporate failures are related not to external factors but to internal corruption. I don't ever want that to happen at Hobby Lobby.

The same goes for any kind of negotiation with a business partner. We need to be people of our word. It is possible to be smart and fair at the same time.

The Government Matters

Another test of our integrity comes in dealing with government authorities, particularly the tax departments. I do not enjoy paying taxes any more than anyone else does, yet the Bible is clear about "rendering unto Caesar" what is due to Caesar, whether we approve of what Caesar does with our money or not.

At Hobby Lobby, we certainly have had our disagreements over the years with the Internal Revenue Service. They got on our case one time about how we were expensing business trips—in that case, trips to research and buy products overseas. Our CFO, Jon Cargill, and his staff argued strongly for a different accounting method. In the end, the IRS refused to budge and we submitted to doing it their way.

When we opened our first store in the state of Michigan in 1999, there were new state rules on business taxation to learn, as with any state. Only after the books had been closed on the first year of operation did one of our tax specialists come to Jon and say, "You know, as I study these regulations more, I think we have been wrong. Looks to me like we owe Michigan around $50,000."

The state revenue department had said nothing at this point. There was no outside demand for payment. That wasn't the main issue to us, though. I remember that Jon said simply, "Well, if we're legally obligated to do this, we'll pay it right away. I'll let David know." And when I heard about it, I backed up his decision on the spot. End of subject. Why? Because it was the right thing to do, and Hobby Lobby is God's company.

We had another situation where our buying office in a foreign country advised us not to worry about the onerous (and probably unfair) tax rules. "Nobody pays full taxes in this country!" they explained. "If you do, your money just goes into the pockets of corrupt politicians."

"Well," I replied, "that's not my problem to solve. We're going to do what the law says, regardless." They shook their heads in wonderment.

After we had filed a few tax returns, that country's tax authority stopped by to audit us. They came to a strange conclusion. "You're paying more taxes than some large corporations," they declared. "You shouldn't be doing this."

"Now, why would a tax agent say something like that?" I asked myself when I heard the story.

I finally figured out the angle. If we started cutting corners like everyone else, they would have grounds to say, "You're cheating the government. We're going to have to take you to court—unless you want to, uh . . . " and the invitation to bribery would begin.

I told our employees later, "Do you see how this kind of behavior is hurting your country? No wonder the roads aren't being fixed and the schools aren't being improved. Too much money is being diverted from what the people actually need."

As business people, we can complain all we want about government—its inefficiencies, its questionable decisions, its overspending—since there's no shortage of fodder these days for that. In the end, though, we need government to do its job.

The Bible says, "It is necessary to submit to the authorities, not only because of possible punishment but also as a matter of conscience. This is also why you pay taxes, for the authorities are God's servants, who give their full time to governing. Give to everyone what you owe them: If you owe taxes, pay taxes; if revenue, then revenue; if respect, then respect; if honor, then honor" (Rom. 13:5–7).

If the apostle Paul could write those words about a government as harsh and pagan as the Roman Empire, I certainly cannot ignore its message regarding Washington and the dozens of states or countries in which I do business.

Whoever follows me in the CEO chair someday is going to be tempted to cut corners. Yet, for me, part of leaving a rich legacy to my family and business means firmly setting a precedent of honest dealings. It is simple. Serve the Lord and do what his Word says is right. Then, no matter what happens, even when the company closes or some other trouble comes along, you can be confident you have God's favor—with something of much greater value to pass on to your children than a billion-dollar company.

Why do we think this way? Because Hobby Lobby is a company owned by the Lord. Even our confidence that this is true is part of the legacy we want to embed in the generations that follow us.

Part 3

GIVING IT ALL AWAY

Stewardship—like humility—requires a recognition that life is not about us.

—Tony Dungy

Nearly every moment of every day we have the opportunity to give something to someone else—our time, our love, our resources. I have always found more joy in giving when I did not expect anything in return.

—S. Truett Cathy

For where your treasure is, there your heart will be also.

—Jesus of Nazareth

Chapter 6

JOURNEY INTO GENEROSITY

You have not lived today until you have done something for someone who can never repay you.

—John Bunyan, Writer and Baptist Preacher

Remember the big ideas of chapter one—our unseen legacy, family, wealth means more than money? At the core of any meaningful life and legacy has to be a vision for generosity, an understanding of what it means to be a blessing for others. The value of giving to church, to missions, to people must first be modeled, then taught so that the next generation embraces generosity as their calling. Once a person embraces a concept, like generosity, as their own, then it's much easier to understand the responsibility attached to it.

My journey into generosity has shown me two important things, among others. First, generosity has a starting point. You don't just wake up one day and *poof*, you're generous. It begins with a decision to steward your resources with a heavenly mindset. Second, generosity depends not on how much money we have but on the posture of our hearts. Too often we think of generosity as the sharing and giving of money. But that's a shallow definition. Generosity goes much deeper.

In this chapter, I want to walk you through bits and pieces of my own journey to show you how I learned the value of generosity and how it can start ever so small, but eventually have massive impact for God's kingdom.

A Note on Perspective

In his excellent little book *The Treasure Principle*, Randy Alcorn gives a vivid word picture about our perspective on generosity:

> Imagine you're alive at the end of the Civil War. You're living in the South, but you are a Northerner. You plan to move home as soon as the war is over.
>
> While in the South, you've accumulated lots of Confederate currency. Now, suppose you know for a fact that the North is going to win the war and the end is imminent. What will you do with your Confederate money?
>
> If you're smart, there's only one answer. You should immediately cash in your Confederate currency for U.S. currency—the only money that will have value once the war is over. Keep only enough Confederate currency to meet your short-term needs.[9]

Alcorn reminds us that our earthly currency has a time limit. Upon Christ's return or upon our death, all our money, as well as our possessions, will be worthless. Alcorn admits there's nothing wrong with money, "as long as you understand its limits." When we understand the temporary nature of this world and all that is in it, it should radically alter how we manage our resources, and our money in particular.

I don't know about you, but I don't want to get caught sitting on stacks of worthless money or heaps of meaningless possessions or mountains of unused resources. I want to put as much as I can into forms that will last for eternity.

Ninety Is Greater Than a Hundred

My journey begins in the cotton fields of my youth, learning the importance of tithing. I count myself fortunate to have received this message early and consistently from my parents. From the first dollar I made picking cotton as a grade-schooler, I was taught to give God ten percent. Our family took Jesus literally when he said, "It is more blessed to give than to receive" (Acts 20:35).

My mother was particularly devoted to tithing. I remember when someone from the church brought our family some food—say a bag of potatoes or some corn—Mother immediately calculated the market value of the gift so she could tithe ten percent. If I heard her say it once, I heard her say it a thousand times: "Honor the Lord with thy substance, and with the first fruits of all thine increase" (Prov. 3:9 KJV).

My parents taught us to obey that verse faithfully.

Based on this early training, Barbara and I never debated whether to tithe on our modest paycheck when we got married. We believed that if we honored God in this way, he would bless us—maybe not financially but in any number of other ways.

When the children came along, we taught them the same principle.

I remember well when Mart and Steve began working in our kitchen gluing picture frames. They carefully computed the tithe on their tiny income and then joyfully put it in the offering plate on Sundays. They were only nine and seven years old when we started our business, but they already understood that even if you were earning only seven cents for making picture frames, ten percent went to God. They never complained about this sacrifice. They were grateful to do it.

To this day, Mart says, "I never thought about *not* tithing. It was just what we did in our house. It was our starting point with regard to money."

As I was growing up, I'd hear my dad say, "Ninety is greater than a hundred."

I remember asking him, "What do you mean by that?"

He replied, "Ninety percent with God is more than a hundred percent without him."

The value of giving to God was embedded in our children from the earliest days.

Simplify: Start Vertically

Now, I'm well aware that tithing is not the practice of every Christian family. We're probably the exception rather than the rule. Regardless, this is a subject worth the attention of us all. And remember, generosity begins with me and you deciding to be good stewards of our resources and the posture of our hearts.

I certainly understand that, for all of us, life and finances have gotten a lot more complex since our childhood days. Our multiple-page tax returns bear witness to that. In today's changing world of the self-employed and the entrepreneur, incomes can come from a variety of sources. Many folks have income streams spread out across a wide variety of categories.

For some it may even be difficult to determine exactly which money is personal and which is business. When people in this situation are challenged to give ten percent, a natural response would be "Ten percent of what?"

Just the complications of it all can produce a gray fog of indecision about giving.

So trust me. I get that it can seem gray. My intention is to help with the clarity. I don't intend to criticize anyone's situation or choices. Instead, I want to focus on what my wife and I consider the central reason for giving: to please God and thank him for sharing his blessings with us.

For our family, giving is a vertical thing that is between us and our Father in heaven. It is not a horizontal thing that is oriented to what other people think about us or how they'll react. Our attitude is the same as the psalmist, who wrote, "What shall I return to the Lord for all his goodness to me?" (Ps. 116:12).

We can almost imagine this man with palms upraised to God, a big smile on his face. He wants to give to the one who has been so generous with him. This is how we feel.

People often say to me, "Well, should you pay tithes on the gross or on the net of your income?" I feel like answering, "You know, just by raising that question, you seem to imply, 'How little can I get away with and still fulfill the rule?'"

I can't imagine Abraham or David asking that question.

I'm not interested in focusing on how little I can give.

Rather, my approach is "How *much* can I give?"

As far as I'm concerned, the tithe, or ten percent, is not a ceiling for giving but, rather, a floor. Beyond that minimum, we move into the zone called "offerings." Barbara and I yearn to give both tithes and offerings with willing hearts. The more we give, the more God blesses us. That's his way.

I'm not saying God has committed to bless us or anyone else dollar-for-dollar. God's command to give is not a transactional formula, despite what some prosperity preachers teach. I believe, instead, that God notices generosity and helps givers keep on growing and giving.

The Adventure of Tithing

And let me tell you, giving like we do is exciting. It's an adventure.

Sitting in church on a Sunday night back in 1997, Barbara and I learned about an outreach to the world's children called Book of Hope. Today it is called OneHope. A speaker that night explained how for just thirty-three cents, they could print and deliver a sixty-four-page color booklet that told the story of Christ's life, death, and resurrection in terms understandable to a child. He said they had invitations to do this in many schools around the globe using volunteer teams.

I went up after the service and talked to the speaker. I invited him to visit me in my office and share details. Eventually, he arranged for Book of Hope's president, Bob Hoskins, to come see me. The meeting went well. I got answers to my questions, and I was impressed with what this program could do to impact the youth of the world and agreed to make a contribution of $2 million.

Here's where it gets interesting. Bob had his meeting with me but did not tell his son Rob about it. Separately, but about the same time, Rob received a request from a missionary in the Philippines who wanted Rob to meet with the minister of education for their country. "I want to try to get the *Book of Hope* in all the Philippine high schools!" the missionary said enthusiastically.

"How many kids would that be?" Rob asked.

"Six million."

Rob did the math in his head. How could they ever raise $2 million for just one country? Still, he agreed to fly to Manila for the meeting with the government official.

The day of the meeting came and the missionary made his pitch. When he was done, the minister of education became very serious. "We appreciate the United States and all you've done for our country," he said. "You helped us rebuild after World War II. We set up our system of education to follow your pattern. But when you took the Bible out of your schools in 1963, we followed suit. So I am denying your request, based on your own government's laws."

In that moment, Rob Hoskins felt agitated. "Sir," he responded, "do you know what has happened to our nation's youth since 1963?" Rob reeled off statistics about the rise in violence, alcohol abuse, drugs, and teen pregnancy, and the drop in SAT scores.

Before long, the government official started commiserating with him! He told statistics of his own, which mirrored the American numbers. Then something odd happened. The official pushed himself back from his desk and called for his secretary. He said he wanted to dictate a letter of permission for the *Book of Hope* to be brought to every Filipino school child.

"Now, I'm going to put my name and my seal on this letter," he said to his two visitors. "Can you really make this happen?"

In that moment, Rob Hoskins's brain said, "There's no way!" But he opened his mouth and answered, "Yes, we can do it."

The missionary almost fell out of his chair. Once outside, he turned worriedly to Rob and said, "Do you know what you just promised? Of course, you'll get on a plane tomorrow, but I have to stay here and live with these people!"

During a plane change in Tokyo on the trip home, Rob called his father in Florida. "I have good news and bad news," he announced. "The good news is that permission has been granted. We have an open door all across the Philippine school network. The bad news is that we need $2 million right away."

The father started laughing on the other end of the line. "Don't fret, son," he said. "Remember that meeting in Oklahoma that I went to? I'm sitting here holding a check in my hand for $2 million!" At this, both men began to weep.

Since that day more than a decade ago, we've continued to

partner with this strategic ministry. I love the impact they are making all around the world. Their vision is simple: "God's Word. Every Child." Their financial model is equally clear: "Three for a dollar." Now that's a concept a retailer can understand! Nearly every member of our family has traveled overseas with them and helped to pass out this life-giving book. We've all been enriched and stretched through the experience.

Adventure!

We took interest in something that resonated with our hearts and dove in. We got involved through the vehicle of finances and have been blessed to have witnessed God do incredible things. It not only resonated with our hearts, but it aligned with our values, vision, and the call we feel God has on our finances. This is why it's so important to develop a plan. (Which I'll demonstrate later in the book.)

$30,000? Really, God?

I can anticipate the questions of some of my fellow business leaders, as well as the seasoned and rookie entrepreneur. I can almost hear them thinking, "Personal giving, even tithing, is a good thing for individuals to do. But why should a corporation give away its hard-earned profits? After all, keeping the bottom line black instead of red these days is hard enough without handing out money just for the fun of it. Wouldn't it be wiser to use whatever earnings I generate to expand my market, to pay down debt, or to reward key personnel?"

I understand these concerns.

Hobby Lobby didn't give corporate donations in its early years either. I said to myself back then, "Maybe later. I need to use every dollar now to grow this business . . . so we can give more down the road." That was my rationalization.

Then around 1979, I was attending a large convention of my

denomination in Tennessee. Missionaries from all over the world gave presentations on their work. I paid close attention, remembering how my mother had always given special care and effort to funding foreign missions.

As I flew home after the meetings, I was looking out the airplane window when something unusual happened. It seemed a quiet voice inside of me said, "You need to give $30,000 for literature." During the convention, one of the speakers had talked about the need for more printed material in his particular field. His words came back to me as I sat on that plane.

My first reaction to the words I sensed in my heart was that $30,000 was far too much money to consider. The company wasn't nearly big enough to afford that amount. We had only four stores. No, I concluded. This is impossible!

Yet the impression wouldn't go away.

"God, I don't have $30,000," I silently prayed. "But you're serious about this, aren't you?" It was just then that I had an idea. "Well, I suppose I could write four checks for $7,500 each, and postdate them a month apart for the next four months."

I sat there pondering this option. Then I did some calculating. Maybe this would work after all.

When I reached home, I wrote the four checks. I then put them in an envelope, took a deep breath, prayed that I could make good on them, and mailed them to Tennessee.

When the church official on the other end called to acknowledge my gift, he made an intriguing comment. "The day your letter was postmarked," he said, "was the very day that four African missionaries had a special prayer meeting for literature funds. Looks like God answered their prayer!"

Something clicked inside me at that moment. My longstanding

uneasiness about not going into the ministry like all my brothers and sisters went away. It settled permanently inside of me that God had a purpose for a businessman. He had called me. He had blessed me. There must be a role for people like me in the work of the kingdom of God.

That was the beginning of Hobby Lobby's participation in God's work. Good times, bad times—it didn't matter. I was determined that this business would play its role in the kingdom of God. In making this decision, I quickly experienced the same joy in giving with my business as I did in my personal life.

Generosity: God's Fuel for the Entrepreneur

Let me say something right here that I believe with all my heart. In all the world there are only two eternal things—the Word of God and the souls of people. All else is temporary, transient, and short-lived. Remember Randy Alcorn's story I shared earlier? To invest in eternal things is the most important thing we can do with our lives, our energies, and our resources. It's vital in our personal lives, and in our business ventures our perspective remains eternal rather than temporal.

From that moment on that airplane in 1979, we have chosen to be a company that gives. Naturally, the amount we give has gotten progressively larger over the years as the company has expanded. I don't begrudge one nickel of it. We've set out to work with organizations that tell people about Christ, from global ministries such as Every Home for Christ to our local city rescue mission.

My personal faith directs my efforts and fuels my passion for generosity. Since I believe there's a real heaven and a real hell, I want to direct as many people toward heaven and away from hell as I can. I want them to know the peace that's available through knowing Christ. God has given us the resources and the partnerships to reach them. I truly believe there will be millions of people in heaven because of this effort.

For me, the question is not, "Why would we use our profits for this?" It is rather, "Why *wouldn't* we use our profits for this?" If we don't use Hobby Lobby's earnings to touch people for the Lord, I really don't see the reason for me to be in business at all.

When to Give

I could tell stories of more wonderful partnerships. From the track record of corporate earnings that is now building year by year, it seems to me that God is smiling on this philosophy of giving. Hobby Lobby has retired all long-term debt and our profits have continued to grow, even throughout the recent recession.

Other business owners may say to me, "Well, that's nice. You're riding high these days, so no wonder you can be generous. My situation is different, however. My industry is struggling, and I'm barely hanging on. I can't afford to give."

My reply is, "This is exactly the time to start giving!" God will notice your heart. To commit yourself to his purposes can get you up and out of your struggle. I know this doesn't sound logical, but in God's eternal economy, it is true.

There's a phrase common in some Christian circles that goes, "You can't out-give God." I tossed around that phrase myself more than once. Then, about thirteen years ago, God seemed to say to me, "Well, you haven't really tried, have you?" That really brought me up short.

I shared this with other family members. As a point of

confirmation, Mart had come up with essentially the same plan. We agreed that Hobby Lobby needed to launch out into whole new ventures of giving. We decided to dramatically increase our giving over the following six months. Then we would increase six months later. We would continue this pattern thereafter. I looked down the road and said to myself, "By the time we get five or six years into this, we won't be able to keep up."

Well, God has proven faithful. We're now giving at a level I previously thought impossible, and we're still going! The more this business gives, the more God blesses us to keep giving.

Like a lot of families, we started with giving to our church. Then we expanded to mission agencies. God keeps bringing us causes bigger than ourselves. Even as the projects grow in size and scope, our business has kept growing. We truly cannot seem to get ahead of him.

It's so easy to rationalize not giving.

We're in a recession.

My business is struggling.

We just had our first child.

I have a mountain of school loans.

I'm about to retire and need the funds.

The list goes on. In my own journey, I've discovered that the timing of generosity reveals your heart to God. That step of writing the check or hitting the "donate" button online can seem daunting. But it all comes down to trust. Do I really trust that God is the same God who stayed Abraham's hand from slaughtering his son and provided a ram in the thicket for the sacrifice? If my answer is yes, then that carries consequences. Good ones, too.

It means that as a consequence of God's provisional faithfulness, I can take joy in giving even in hard times. Oftentimes, God just wants us to take the first step. It can be as simple as making a plan to get out of debt or a plan to support a missionary family for a decade. It's the first step. Once we commit, I've found that God is quick to reveal himself in that endeavor.

When to give? I humbly suggest *always.*

We give with joy in our hearts.

We give out of our humble circumstances.

We give out of our wealth.

It doesn't matter whether we give out of wealth or humble circumstances. God can't wait for us to step into the joy of generosity. We just need to trust him and take that first step.

Chapter 7

THE JOY OF GIVING

It's not how much we give but how much love we put into giving.

—MOTHER TERESA, ROMAN CATHOLIC NUN

I ONCE HEARD IT SAID that everyone wants to receive a miracle, but no one wants to be in a position to receive one. So it is with learning the joy of giving. We want to experience the joy without taking the step of faith to get there.

For most of us, the giving journey is evolutionary. I didn't start out giving 50 percent. My giving started out with watching my parents give. It grew as I practiced it with Barbara and our children. I took a big leap forward when I gave $30,000 I knew I didn't have.

I remember a number of years ago now I was thinking a bit out loud, "You can't out-give God!" At that point, it seemed that God nudged me and said, "Well, you've never really tried." And from then on the adventure has really taken off.

I remember praying and working on a plan to dramatically increase our giving that called for us to increase our giving every six months. When I presented the plan to the family, I discovered Mart had come up with the same faith-stretching plan. So that's what we began working on—a plan to out-give God. We can't out-give God, of course. Today, we've landed on giving roughly 50 percent of our profits. But we continue to pray and rely on the Holy Spirit for guidance.

But that giving has also meant looking for other ways to be creative in our giving. For instance, we've given real estate as a way to help particular ministries. Mart and Steve give their time and expertise to the ministries they work with. For my part, even though I don't like public speaking, I've taken on more of these events than I ever could have imagined.

We've engaged in projects that are world changing in scope, and things I never could have dreamed of forty years ago. For instance, we've had the opportunity to support the work of Every Tribe Every Nation, whose goal is to make the Bible available in every language in the world. This effort is unique because it involves the cooperation of several organizations and is working to speed Bible translation efforts.

We've also had the opportunity to be part of efforts to establish the Museum of the Bible in Washington, D.C. This museum will invite all people to engage with the Bible. Never before in our country's history have we had a national Bible museum, even though so much of our history is based on it. It is scheduled to open in 2017.

One of my favorite ministries is Every Home for Christ, led by Dick Eastman. This ministry gives me great confidence because Dick and his wife, Dee, are great prayer warriors. I know that their ministry is bathed in prayer. I like Every Home for Christ because of their work in planting churches all around the world. They are going door-to-door handing out literature in 130 nations.

Why do I mention all of these things? None of these adventures would have been possible if I didn't take the first step. So I encourage you and challenge you to take the next step. Maybe it's a first step. Maybe it's a bolder step.

No More Giving Excuses

When we give to God, we allow God to "open the floodgates of heaven" (Mal. 3:10). Some Christians, I'm afraid, see the opposite. They think they'll wind up with less if they give. I see it in terms of future blessings. I need and want God's blessings on our family. As I give, it seems that he showers us with more and more blessings.

Some Christians use the excuse, "Well, you know, the money might not be used wisely. I'm not really confident that the church or some other ministry organization will make good decisions on what to do with these funds."

To these people I say, "Then find someplace that will show good stewardship." Go online and check out what the Evangelical Council for Financial Accountability or Charity Navigator has to say about those ministries. Look for a project or ministry that God seems to be blessing. That's what we do, both in our personal giving and at the corporate level. There are plenty of churches and ministries that are doing solid work and being good stewards of their funds.

Let's stop finding excuses not to give. Instead, let's discover the avenues for giving that God has placed in our lives and tackle them with all the might of our generosity.

With so many options to give in our advanced society, you'd think that giving would be off the charts. The truth is that we need to walk in the ways of our grandparents. Studies reveal that in the 1930s, church members gave 3.2 percent of their incomes. That was during the Great Depression. Today, with our much higher earning levels, the percentage of giving is only 2.6 percent.[10] It is time for our generation to rethink our giving habits. I believe the best way to do this is to consider the great benefits of the promises of God.

I'm not saying we should pray that God will open the floodgates of heaven so that we can get money back. That way of thinking does not align with God's. There's more to God's blessing than money. We need to rid ourselves of this mindset that focuses on mountains of money. God's provision for our lives can come in the form of assistance from the body of Christ (people from your church) or in the form of a gift of some kind, a job opportunity. My mother gave obediently and joyfully, and God provided. She didn't get rich as the world defines it, but she built up treasure in heaven while she trusted God to provided for her in the here and now.

For the Joy

As I consider my giving journey, the thing that has surprised me the most is how much joy it has brought me. I never could have imagined the people or the places that I would see. I never could have imagined all the lives that would be impacted. That brings me joy and peace that is hard to quantify.

My son Mart likes to quote Chip Ingram, who says, "Generosity is a gateway into intimacy with God."[11] And that's the big thing: God is a giver. We were made in his image, and when we act like him, we become like him.

In Hebrews 12:2, the writer says of Jesus, "for the *joy* set before him he endured the cross." Joy and giving go together. I think the most satisfied and joyful person in heaven will be Jesus as he looks around at all those who have been saved from a life of misery.

Let me make my plea to you. Take God at his word. Test him. I'm convinced that if you take a step and keep moving forward on the adventure of giving, there is no way that you'll be disappointed.

As you've heard me mention before, my mother was my hero when it came to giving. She gave her all—from dresses to doilies to vegetables to her few coins. My sister was with my mother when she passed away. At the time of my mother's passing, she sat up with vigor to her voice as she cried out, "Do you see them? Do you see them?" At first, my sister was puzzled, but she realized that a company of angels had come to take my mother home.

I believe that any billionaire would pay to trade places with my mother to experience that joy.

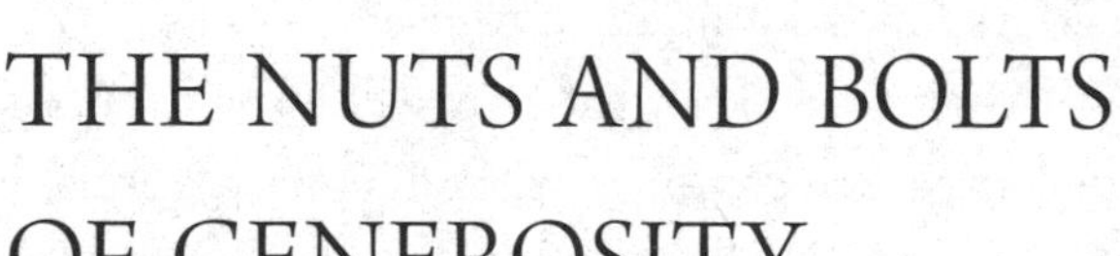

Chapter 8

THE NUTS AND BOLTS OF GENEROSITY

One gives freely, yet grows all the richer; another withholds what he should give, and only suffers want.

—The Teacher, the book of Proverbs

"Great, David. I'm there with you. I'm trusting God with my resources, especially my money. But after the church, where should I give? And how much?"

I hear you. In this chapter I've compiled a kind of field guide to giving. It's how we approach it as a family.

You might be stuck trying to decide where to give your resources and how much to give. These are important considerations for us all at any age. You don't want to give to an organization that mismanages funds. In the next two sections, I want to briefly give you six insights into how we decide where and how much to give. I want to encourage you in your giving and perhaps to ignite some ideas for you.

The first three are principles about how to identify targets and yardsticks for giving, and they apply to individuals and businesses alike. The second three are questions about how to give and what will happen in the future. These questions focus more on generational family giving. I share a bit of the nuts and bolts of how our family decides which organizations to give to.

My hope is that what I say will inspire you, whether you're an early stage entrepreneur, a married couple, a seasoned business owner, or a soon-to-be college graduate. So let your mind play a bit, and see whether God ignites your heart with the fire of generosity.

Where to Give?

1. Set Your Criteria

As you might imagine, we've had to develop some criteria about where to place our gifts. There's no lack of people and organizations knocking on our door for help. Our criteria come out of what I said earlier about the biggest issue of all for us: eternal destiny. We base our giving decisions on whether the result will be some spiritual change in a person's life, directly or indirectly.

Think of a scale from one to ten. Whenever people come to Christ, we consider that a ten. That's why I love the organizations that lead people to Jesus. Training Christians to go out and lead people to Christ is a nine for me. That's the reason we got involved with several Christian colleges, for example. They're training students to go out into the world as lights for Christ.

On the other hand, the local Boy Scouts or the chamber of commerce are good causes, but they're not a number nine on our list. We don't mind supporting good things in our community, but this kind of giving is not the central reason we exist. We seek to invest God's profits in things that will make a real difference for eternity.

I've mentioned two new projects that are very exciting and reflect our giving criteria. One is called Every Tribe Every Nation (www

.everytribeeverynation.com). Every Tribe Every Nation's goal is to get God's Word to every person on earth. The second big project is the Museum of the Bible (www.museumofthebible.org). This is a world-class museum in the heart of Washington, D.C.

Our decision to give to these organizations, among others, remains linked to our overarching mission to support organizations that are telling people about the love of Jesus Christ through God's Word. This is our criteria for giving.

So I've told you our focus. What's yours?

If you know it, pull out the notes app on your smart phone or open your journal and jot down your primary giving criteria. If you've not given it much thought, I encourage you to sit down with your family or business and pray about the direction God wants you to give. Rather than shotgunning resources all over the place, consider that there is much joy to be found in directing your efforts toward a certain area. It's so exciting for us to see our efforts build into such a wonderful impact on the lives of so many folks.

2. Set Your Giving Amount

The ideas in this section can apply either to an individual or to a business owner. From the business perspective, the amount of money we have to give is, of course, dependent on the earnings of Hobby Lobby. A target these days is for us to give away roughly half of our earnings. The government actually allows people to deduct up to 50 percent of their income each year; we are inclined to take advantage of that opportunity. We view it as wise stewardship to use all of the deduction we can, particularly because that increased giving level allows us to see more impact in the world through our giving.

The other half of our profits, understandably, goes toward growing the business—starting up more stores, making infrastructure improvements, and investing in other profitable ventures. The better payoffs we get from these things, the more we can plow into giving toward God's work. Again, the point is not to enrich any of us personally. The point is to be generous with what God has given.

From an individual perspective, don't underestimate the power of making a plan and writing it down. Remember what I said earlier about taking first steps with God? Sit down with your parents or your spouse or your family and make a giving goal. You might say something like, "On top of giving my tithe to the church (ten percent), I want to give an additional five percent of my income away. And every year I want to increase that percentage by one percent." That's a great plan! Write it down and do it.

3. Set a Fire for the Future

Touching a torch to your generosity is obviously not the way a lot of business owners think today. Even Christian business owners find this approach to giving challenging. The reality is our collective national thought concerning generosity has shifted. Our financial planning adviser wrote not long ago in the *Christian Research Journal* that "the facts tell us that we've fallen short in our teaching and theology of money. The facts tell us that the largest givers in our history, the World War II Generation, are heading toward death and retirement and will be replaced by a generation of non-givers. The facts tell us that the current social and political climates don't bode well for giving."[12]

We are determined not to let the fire of generosity die out at Hobby Lobby. As long as God sees fit to prosper this company, we're going to keep giving back to God's work. Naturally, we want this God-given purpose to live in the next generation. This is part of the legacy we want to leave, not only in the amount of money we have generated (seen legacy) but in the commitment to give as God gives (unseen legacy), a commitment which we believe has led to all of our wealth in the first place.

We believe that if we can lead in the way that we give, then we can inspire people from all walks of life to take up the mantle of generosity.

Generosity is about more than money. A generous spirit shapes us as individuals. We live with a perspective that differs from our consumer driven society. A generous spirit affects how we use our time, those we seek to help in our community and abroad, how willing we are to serve in our church gatherings. We want to display Jesus' character in how we give and inspire others to be generous too.

We want to be part of a new generation of givers. Personally, I want to see my children and grandchildren affect this world through their generous hearts. I believe that journey begins when we take the first step and commit to giving ten percent to God, then join him on the pathway of generosity. Once we begin the journey, we discover how vast and nuanced are the blessings of God.

Generosity quickly becomes contagious. I imagine there are some reading these words who are eager to get started on their own journey of giving. Let me warn you that developing practical systems of giving is essential. Effective giving cannot be done on an emotional basis alone. You'll need some criteria for choosing recipients, such as our one-to-ten rating scale, and you'll need to set a target on how much to disperse that is something like our half-of-profits guideline.

Following are three other questions for you to think about concerning how to give.

How to Give

1. Give Directly or Indirectly?

Will you deal directly with the ministries and other charities to which you give? Or will you stay in the shadows and use some means of conveyance? Warren Buffett, as most of the world now knows, has decided to channel his giving through the Bill and Melinda Gates Foundation, since he agrees with their priorities for fighting poverty and disease around the world. There are a number of Christian foundations that provide a similar pipeline for wealthy individuals to use as well.

The Green family has chosen not to go that route. We've opted to be hands-on in our giving. We meet the folks actually doing the ministry, read their proposals, evaluate the merits of their work, and even counsel them on how they might more efficiently use the available dollars. One of my grandsons, Tyler, used to serve full time as our ministries coordinator. Tyler has now passed that baton to a new coordinator. The ministries coordinator briefs the rest of the family in a monthly meeting in which we make the final decisions about all giving.

This approach is a bit more time consuming, yet we find it invigorating. It's exciting to see what God is doing through these various organizations, to read their reports, and to come alongside their leaders as they strategize for growth and impact. I'm always glad we're in the loop with them.

2. Who Decides?

The power to say, "Okay, let's give X amount to this applicant," or, "No, let's not," is huge, of course. If you're the founder of your enterprise, you may have the right to make these decisions alone. Yet as a wise, rich man once wrote, "Plans fail for lack of counsel, but with many advisers they succeed" (Prov. 15:22). In our family, we've said that if we're all meant to tend this one big, fruitful tree called Hobby Lobby, then we need to come together and help decide what to do with the harvest.

Seated around the conference table on the first Wednesday of every month are seven people: Barbara, our son Mart, our son Steve, our daughter, Darsee, her husband, Stan Lett, our nephew Randy Green, and me. The seven of us hold an equal vote.

We start out every meeting with scripture reading and prayer. Then we make a list of funding requests that have come our way over the previous month. Most of these have come from the giving coordinator's desk, but others may have come through any of the rest of us. These are not the whole number of requests by any means. The number of requests can run as high as three hundred a month. The giving coordinator screens the applicants that don't fit our criteria, as do the rest of us. In this meeting, we concentrate only on those we might actually support.

The name of each candidate organization is written on a whiteboard. Then comes the now familiar question: "Okay, is anyone an advocate for this? Does anyone feel strongly enough to take up the cause and make a case for this organization?" If no one raises a hand, that's the end of the discussion. We don't spend any more time on that name.

Then we continue with a more careful look at those that remain. We get "down into the weeds," as I like to say. We probe for details.

- Is this project feasible?
- Can they pull it off if we give them the money?
- Or is this just a wistful idea?
- Is this organization well managed?
- How much debt are they carrying?

- Are they accredited with an outside agency such as the Evangelical Council for Financial Accountability?
- Will this project truly advance the work of the kingdom of God?

We each have our favorite ministries, naturally. What we hope for, though, is a seven-person consensus. The discussion may take a while. We don't vote until our hearts are settled. I especially have to be careful not to lobby too hard for my opinion, even though I am "the dad." Yes, my family members naturally defer to me, and I appreciate it, but I really do want to know what they are thinking. They might see a flaw that I'm missing.

Finally, I'll say, "Okay, are we ready to vote? They're requesting $250,000," or whatever the amount is. Everyone has a pad of yellow sticky notes. "Write down what you would see us giving, any number from zero up to 250,000." I then collect the notes and see what we've got. It's supposed to be a secret ballot, except that Darsee—the artistic one—can't seem to keep from doodling on her ballot, thus giving away her identity!

If the range of recommendations is split, we negotiate with each other. Usually, we land somewhere in the middle. The final decision is written down and conveyed to the applicant. Then, we move on to the next cause.

Before the meeting wraps up, we often spend a few minutes hearing reports of how our past giving has played out—the people who came to Christ as a result or how a certain building is working out. It's a time of rejoicing for us to see what God has done.

This monthly process is not a burden to us by any means. It's one of the more enjoyable meetings we have. I think it's wonderfully healthy.

Here's what one trio of authors says about choosing a method:

> As you make decisions about when and where and how much of your wealth you will invest in Kingdom work, how will you involve your family? By involving your loved ones in your decisions, you will be teaching them that their Master owns it all. You will model what it means to manage what isn't yours in the first place. How will you include them in the decisions as well as the delight? Will you include them in the sacrifice as well as the satisfaction? And how will you strategize for this kind of impact in their lives after you're gone?
>
> As you show them the way to be a "good and faithful servant" who doesn't bury God's gifts, but invests them, you will invite them to the party where they'll hear: "Come and share your master's happiness."[13]

3. How Will Generosity Become Generational?

It is important to ask the question, "What's going to happen after my death? Will the coming generations keep giving as I have?"

I would feel terrible if Hobby Lobby's giving to God's work turned out to be only "Grandpa and Grandma's thing." Toward that end, we are already inviting G3, our grandchildren, to sit in on the monthly giving meetings. They don't yet have a vote, but they get to watch how we decide things, what drives us, and how we negotiate differences of opinion. They see us approve some appeals and reject others and in this way they absorb our values.

We've even taken this a step farther by allocating a certain modest amount of money for them to give away each year. They hold a regular group meeting of their own, without anyone from G1 or G2 in the room. It's up to them to evaluate proposals and decide whether to give.

In this way, they're getting practice for the future when the amounts to be given away will be much larger.

Tyler moderates this meeting with his siblings and cousins. Not all G3s can attend every meeting. Some are away at college and some are still underage, but Tyler works to keep the group as cohesive as possible. They're finding out that giving away money in a responsible manner is harder than it looks. That's all right. It's a good education for what's ahead. They are learning the process of doing something together that has eternal value.

How you choose to organize your giving is, as I said at the beginning of this chapter, a personal decision. Make sure the results are what you want to happen, both now and for decades to come.

Part 4

THE LEGACY OF WORK AND FAMILY

In short, work—and lots of it—is an indispensable component in a meaningful human life. It is a supreme gift from God and one of the main things that gives our lives purpose. But it must play its proper role, subservient to God. It must regularly give way not just to work stoppage for bodily repair but also to joyful reception of the world and of ordinary life.

—Timothy Keller

Those who work their land will have abundant food,
but those who chase fantasies have no sense.

—The Teacher

Stay calm; mind your own business; do your own job. You've heard all this from us before, but a reminder never hurts. We want you living in a way that will command the respect of outsiders, not lying around sponging off your friends.

—Paul the Apostle

Chapter 9

THE LEGACY OF WORK

We often miss opportunity because it's dressed in overalls and looks like work.

—Thomas A. Edison, Inventor

The moment has come for me to say some difficult things about legacy, about work, about character, and about how we should approach the next generation. It is important for you to know that I share these truths not out of anger or fear or any personal disappointment. Instead, I believe that there are some time-honored principles that we need to reclaim in our day.

Some will say that David Green has gone old school in this chapter. That's okay. I actually am old school. But not so old to realize that when I was young I benefited from the wisdom of the old-schoolers. So I'll own it. I am going old school, but only because there are some things the old-schoolers used to teach that we need now. I offer these insights only in love and only with a desire to see our generation do our best for the generations yet to come. I mean, I may be old school now, but I still have heart.

Through the years, Barbara and I have often said to each other,

"When you have wealth, the hardest thing to do for your kids is not to do." Everything within you wants to whip out your checkbook or your credit card and bail them out of their troubles. You love them. You want to help. Yet rescuing them in this way is exactly what will cripple them. Perhaps you watch them scraping up money at a minimum-wage job to buy their first car. It makes you cringe. Yet you know that you can't intervene. They are learning the value of work, one of the most important lessons life has to teach.

Barbara and I have had to say this to our kids and grandkids: "We love you dearly. Part of that love is to arrange things so that you get only what you earn by working. We're going to give you something greater than wealth, which is opportunity. You are most welcome to work at Hobby Lobby if you wish, provided you do a good job like anyone else. Then you can enjoy the fruit of your labor. But the ownership of this company is a whole different matter, which we need to talk about."

I remember an incident early in my working career, before we even launched our own company. I watched as the late-twenties son of a woman on my sales staff showed up in the store one day to ask his mom for money. She went to get her purse and handed him a couple of bills.

Something bothered me about this. I said to her afterward, "You're not making that much yourself. Don't you need that money for your own needs?"

"But . . . but that's my son!" she replied with a wistful tone.

I was dismayed. In truth, that mother needed to make her adult son stand on his own two feet. Just as all of us parents do.

The apostle Paul wrote to one church, "When we were with you, we gave you this rule: 'The one who is unwilling to work shall not eat'" (2 Thess. 3:10).

I happen to think this verse applies even to someone who has a large trust fund. God put us here to work. He invented work long ago in the garden of Eden. Even before the fall, Adam and Eve were given the assignment to take care of the garden—to be fruitful and multiply.

Work is not a curse. It is our calling. We should keep working as long as we're able.

Fred Smith Sr. was a Texas business legend and board member of several Christian organizations who taught a large Sunday school class at a major Dallas church. One day after class, a woman approached him with a prayer request. "Would you please pray for my son? He's done with college now, and he's just trying to find the will of the Lord for his life."

"Well, sure," said Smith, "I'll pray for him. What's he doing now? Is he working?"

"No, he's just taking some time off," the mother replied, "waiting for God to show him his will."

Next question from the teacher: "Is he eating?"

The woman looked puzzled as she answered, "Oh, yes. He's staying at our place for the time being."

"Okay, you go home and tell him he's already out of the will of God!" Smith replied with a grin. "The Bible says that if a man doesn't work, neither shall he eat. So he's already out of line with what God said."

I totally agree.

My Life Motto

The will of God for you and me, and your kids and my kids, is clearly stated in Ecclesiastes 9:10: "Whatever your hand finds to do, do it with all your might."

I've taken this as my assignment from the beginning. Whatever work we find ourselves doing in this life—I don't care if it's flipping burgers—we are called to do it well and to the glory of God. The Bible tells us that promotion comes from God, not from human bosses. If you're not doing your best at flipping burgers as you wait for something better, I doubt that you'll ever find your dreams.

We dare not cheat our children out of the experience of work. We must expect that they give it their full energy. We cannot let our personal or corporate reserves undermine this crucial lesson.

I worked thirteen years for other employers before starting Hobby Lobby, and I gave it all I had. As a result, I got promoted repeatedly. Now, I don't believe for a minute that McLellan's or TG&Y gave me those promotions. God did it. As the King James version of the Bible puts it, "Promotion cometh neither from the east, nor from the west, nor from the south. But God is the judge: He putteth down one, and setteth up another" (Ps. 75:6–7).

Those early settings were preparation for my years of leading Hobby Lobby. This is one of the great lessons of life. God uses our work in the insignificant things to fashion our character for the time of our greater destiny.

What might God want to do through the life and talents of your child or your grandchild? You probably won't know if you shortcircuit their experience in working.

Yes, I know the feeling of guilt that comes over us when we watch them struggling financially. It's hard not to jump in and ease the pain. If we do, though, we will stunt their development.

The wealth we create is like a bonfire. If controlled, it can warm our families. If allowed to spread wildly, it can devastate. This is what's happening all too often within wealthy families around the world these days.

One successful businessman said to me with obvious concern,

"I've got forty-four different 'hooks' into my company." By this he meant forty-four different expectations from children, grandchildren, and great-grandchildren. Each of them had their name on some document and was just waiting to cash in. Their mindset was, "So what is my part worth, and when do I get it?"

At the moment, I have ten grandchildren and nine great-grandchildren, with more likely to come along. Every one of them needs to go out into the world, whether at Hobby Lobby or somewhere else, and be productive. God didn't put any of us on this earth merely to sit on a yacht. He put us here to tend the garden he assigned to us. If we want to impart a legacy of generosity, then we must never forget the value of work and its effect on our lives. But discussing work often leads to discussing money, and no one likes to talk about money, right?

Let's Talk about Money

One of the great needs in families is to talk with one another about money and the responsibility it brings. I believe this is a rule of thumb. No matter what tax bracket you call home, you must *talk* about money. Talking about money with our children helps establish a clear understanding of how money works—how to spend it, save it, and pass it on.

In too many wealthy families, money is almost a hush-hush topic, like sex. Everybody knows it exists, but they get nervous having a conversation about it. This leaves room for assumptions and misunderstandings, which can result in bad planning and hurt feelings.

I'm aware of an older man who, having grown up in the Great Depression, has always kept financial matters close to the vest. He has built quite a net worth with a variety of assets. But he still lives in fear of running out—a holdover from his childhood. He hasn't invested in technology. He doesn't use technology in the business and still keeps a six-days-a-week work schedule.

His kids work in the business and haven't gone out to seek other jobs. They assume they'll inherit the business someday. Yet nothing has ever been said about this. They are using up their most productive years waiting for "someday." Meanwhile, Dad keeps showing up at the office every day in a suit and tie. He may live to be a hundred—who knows?

How much better it would be for everyone if this man would talk to his family and make his plans known. How much better for expectations to be communicated. It is something we all have to make a priority. If a child or grandchild doesn't understand our reasoning, get to the bottom of it. Communicate! Preserve the relationship at all costs. Be fair. These steps will help the baton pass safely down the line.

Talking about money is important because it helps set expectations. For the Green family, there is no free ride. We talk about money and also what it means to earn money.

Following are three key subjects that relate to the value of work, for our family and for any family.

1. Earn Your Way

Barbara and I have not promised any of our family members a job at Hobby Lobby. We have said they are welcome to apply, with the understanding that they'll have to perform like anyone else. There's no "tenure" just for being a Green.[14]

I'm aware that some experts in the field of family business transition discourage the hiring of a family member right out of high school or college. Sybil Ferguson, who founded the Diet Center franchise around the same time we started, says with hindsight that a relative ought to work somewhere else for at least two years before coming aboard. David Bork, a seasoned consultant, gets even more specific: three to five years in one or more jobs requiring competence, skill, and sustained performance, with at least one of those jobs lasting at least two years and resulting in at least one promotion. Only then does Bork recommend hiring the young person to work within the family business.

We haven't taken that route. Still, I wouldn't argue against it. I agree that it's important not to get into a rush or build expectations that haven't been justified by observation. We do our kids and grandkids no favors setting them up for failure.

2. Stewardship: Taking Care of What You Work For

Stewardship is simply taking care of what you have and what you work for. It's looking after the things we've been given.

As I've stated throughout this book, I simply don't believe that unearned money helps grow the kind of responsible, motivated, focused offspring we all desire. We simply must raise kids and grandkids to be independent. Otherwise, we make cripples out of them.

I don't want any family member to have a choice on whether to work. Every one of them needs to go to work. I will not take that incentive from them.

Our son Mart recalls, "In high school, I was disappointed that my dad wouldn't buy Steve and me a car. I did manage to get a car at age sixteen, thanks to the fact that I'd been working and saving since I was nine! Dad may have given me a little money for the purchase, but not much.

"It was 1977, and he took me to a car auction. I bought a banana yellow '73 Ford Mustang convertible, one of the last convertibles they made for a while. It looked cool, but it didn't turn out to be such a wise choice. With that rear-wheel drive, it was horrible on snow. I got rid of it fairly quickly, switching to a front-wheel drive Honda."

Mart goes on to make an interesting observation: "Looking around at my high school and college friends, I could just about tell you which ones had paid for their car themselves by how they drove it! You take better care of something you worked for."

One of our grandkids told me that their school friends made an interesting remark after seeing his older, high-mileage car: "What's up? Are you on the 'outs' with your family or something?" These friends assumed that any of the Green clan would be provided with the newest and greatest. No, that isn't how it works.

Barbara and I love our family and want to share with them. We'll probably leave each of them a modest amount in our will, but certainly not enough to float a lifestyle. We never want to be viewed as the heroes of G3, our grandchildren. We stand behind their own parents, G2, who carry the primary responsibility to shape their children. We don't want to usurp their parents' authority and influence.

If we ever think about doing something financially for one of the grandchildren, we consult with the parents first. We'll say, for example, "What if we paid for a third of their college if you, the parents, pay a third and the kid earns a third?" We try to stay in the shadows.

There is one thing we've arranged that might be considered a family perk. We've created an investment fund in Hobby Lobby for any family member who wants to open an account. They can put their money into the company and earn 8.5 percent, which is better than savings accounts are paying these days.

Most of G3 have taken advantage of this. So they can say they are minority investors in the family business. Yet the capital is money they've earned themselves, not anything that was handed to them.

The bottom line is this: no family member, of whatever generation, must ever view Hobby Lobby as his or her source of well-being for all of life. God is our source! He is more than enough for all of us. If we keep our eyes on him and stay lined up with his purposes, we'll be all right. We can confidently go about our daily work, knowing God is our provider and accepting his invitation to do the job he's provided for us.

3. The Character of a Worker, the Heart of a Leader

Now we come to the subject of succession. I'm asked about this frequently. People want to know who's going to be the next CEO of Hobby Lobby.

The answer is I don't know yet, but I do know what kind of person needs to follow me in this office. I'm not exclusively looking for a Green. I'm looking for a worker who displays high character, a deep heart, and a generous spirit.

When our children were younger, Barbara and I assumed one of them would take the reins someday. They are each doing a wonderful job today in various parts of the company, but as I look at their gifts and abilities, it doesn't look like it would be a wise choice to force one of them into my role.

The same is true of G3, at least from what I've seen so far. They're coming along nicely in certain specialized positions within the company, but raising one of them artificially to become the chief of IT or accounting would not be wise. I've seen other companies pick leaders prematurely, before they have a good sense of what the world looks like through their customers' eyes. Disasters usually result. Sometimes in business, you have to do things that are good for customers that don't seem good on a spreadsheet. Only experience can teach this.

So whenever I step aside, family connections will not be the primary consideration in choosing my successor. The needs of the business will come first. Hobby Lobby's health must be protected. After all, it provides employment for thirty thousand people, and it supports a ton of ministry work.

I've told my family members, "If you want to follow me, go into a store and work from the ground up. Become a good assistant manager, then a great manager. Eventually become a district manager, and if you excel at that, you can become a regional vice-president and from there rise to the post of operations VP here in the home office. That's the ladder you should climb."

The way I look at it, a person who does my job needs three things, in this order:

1. Integrity
2. The attitude of a servant
3. A thorough knowledge of the job

If something drastic happens to me tomorrow, I've already given Mart a list of names from our executive ranks whom I'd recommend for certain positions. Still, I'm leaving the decision open to what God shows the family.

If I'm allowed to be here for another ten or fifteen years, that list could change, of course. I might step into a chairman emeritus role at some point down the line, opening up the CEO position for the very best person, regardless of their last name.

Will the next CEO do things exactly the way I have done them? Probably not, but I expect that person to hold to the principle on which this business was founded, which is hard work that results in generosity for the work of God.

There may be new ways to achieve that result. A member of G3 recently raised an interesting question, using the metaphor of Hobby

Lobby as a fruitful apple tree. "What if, somewhere down the road," this grandchild speculated, "we were to swap the apple tree for a cherry tree instead—or a potato patch?" What if we exchanged arts-and-crafts retailing for some other line of business that would produce equal or greater profits for God's purposes?

I'm open to that, so long as the ministry of giving stays intact. The future details of our business in the American marketplace cannot be fully known now. Nevertheless, the mission of our calling must remain steady. God has blessed us for a reason, and we dare not forget it.

Barbara and I are not nervous about the future. We've done the best we can in setting up parameters for those who will follow us. We say with the apostle Paul, "We have this treasure in jars of clay to show that this all-surpassing power is from God and not from us" (2 Cor. 4:7). We look forward to doing our best to helping our family stay rich from one generation to the next in the sense that matters in God's eternal kingdom.

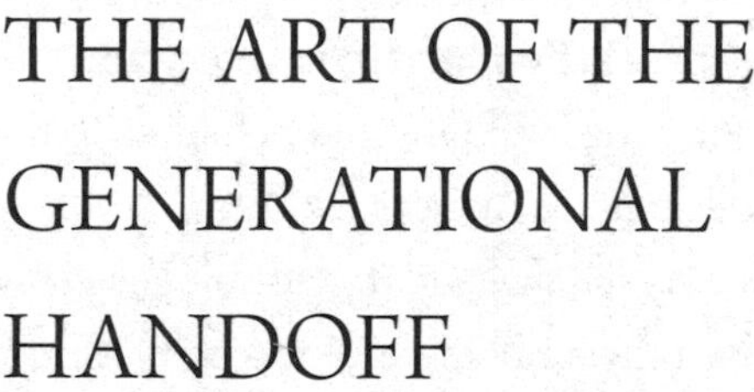

Chapter 10

THE ART OF THE GENERATIONAL HANDOFF

One generation shall commend your works to another, and shall declare your mighty acts.

—King David, Warrior Poet

I think we as a culture have gotten away from the value of family. My upbringing was focused on family. That's all we had. So it mattered. Same with my marriage. My marriage was important enough to *work* at it. I was committed to that.

When I was young, it was impressed upon me that you must do things so that you can keep your family together. That might include celebrating holidays or taking group vacations or having monthly gatherings—that's what we do. Be as creative as you want, the point is you must really make it a priority.

Family matters to me, so you'll understand how conflicted I became when smart money managers told me that I should set up a way to pass wealth to my kids and grandkids. But that made no sense. I knew I needed a plan, but I also knew that money does not last.

It can be squandered.

It can corrupt.

It can blind you to what matters most in this world.

But the values that we ingrain into our family last beyond even death. When I'm gone I want my grandchildren to think of who I was as a person, not about the money I left them.

I want my kids and their kids to see how I used my gifts and God's blessing to serve others, not myself. Jesus emphasized the importance of serving and loving one another, about dying to self and following him down a narrow path. He didn't talk about the importance of ambition, career advancement, or wealth acquisition.

The overarching metaphor in the Bible is family. God is pursuing the "family of God" through his son, Jesus. I want my kids and grandkids to see me working, to see me at the office during working hours, to be able to ask me for advice, to be able to spend time with me. They need to see their grandfather making time for family, not limiting family time for the pursuit of money.

Blessings of a Family Plan

I never thought I'd see a day when three generations of Greens would be sitting around a table discussing generosity. It does something to you deep inside to see your children and their children share the same values and heart for God. Not a day goes by that I don't thank God for this blessing.

All that you have read thus far in this book shows the blessing of God upon Hobby Lobby and the lessons of God for the Green family. These blessings and lessons make up our legacy. It's a legacy that arises from a pastor's home in some of the small towns of America. It was born of the prayers of my parents. It took flight as I fell in love with the retail business, married Barbara, and began a life with her of generosity in obedience to God. It was fashioned both in hard times and in seasons of blessing, in the valleys and on the soaring mountain peaks. Always, it was sustained by the God who owns Hobby Lobby and who ordains that the company be used for his purposes alone.

I believe with all of my heart that these are the reasons—along with the good business sense God also gave us—that Hobby Lobby is as successful as it is. It was God's idea. It is God's company. It was only entrusted to the Green family. Our job has been to lead it to the best of our ability in a manner that honors Jesus Christ and touches as many lives as possible for eternity.

Since all of this is true, perhaps you can understand the depth of the crisis I found myself in during the 1990s. You recall that I described having sleepless nights over the great weight of the wealth we were reaping from the company. It was the crisis that God answered by telling me that he owns Hobby Lobby.

That clear revelation solved a problem I was wrestling with in those days. I want to tell you about that problem and then show you how we resolved it. This really is the heart of what I'm trying to convey in this book, because the problem I was wrestling with had to do with the best way to transfer wealth to the next generation.

Now, before I continue, I understand that the idea of wealth transfer might sound a bit odd to some of you. So allow me a word to bring its importance into focus. First, I want to discuss this notion of transferring wealth from one generation to another because, on a very real level, when done poorly it can have disastrous effects on families whose businesses shape the fabric of our society.

For me, I imagine mountains of money with no plan other than to simply pass it on to the next in line. No safeguards, no guardrails. We need only to turn on the television or hop on the internet to see the monstrous effects great wealth can have on people who possess no moral compass, no compassion for others, and only a desire to get rich and stay rich.

But the same is true for heads of families who will pass on any kind of wealth to their children. It's all about safeguards. If those are not in place, then the next generation will struggle to keep the family vision intact.

The second reason I want to discuss wealth transfer is to use it for a broader, more universal purpose. In this regard, the notion of wealth transfer serves as a metaphor, an example of the great impact constructing a family vision can have on your immediate family and the generations that follow you.

Transferring wealth or the wisdom of a family vision from one generation to the next can be tricky. But it can be done successfully if a vision is in place. A vision for the Green family carries philanthropic, ethical, and spiritual implications. I believe it's the same for you.

To explain this problem and to try to teach lessons from how we solved it, I need to tell you a bit about the wealth that Hobby Lobby was producing by the 1990s. I trust you will recognize that I am only stating facts and that I do it for the good of the message of this book.

How Wealth Can Divide

Beginning in the 1990s, Hobby Lobby made huge profits. Over the years, this has totaled billions of dollars. Every year now, I am listed on the *Forbes* magazine elite list called the Forbes 400, the magazine's list of the wealthiest people in America. I have asked the Forbes people to keep me off of their list, but they refuse to listen. Still, my inclusion on this list will give you some sense of the great abundance God has given us by blessing Hobby Lobby.

The truth is that we are one of the most profitable companies in America. You can find larger companies. You can find better-known companies or companies that are more global. Yet you would be challenged to find a more profitable company than we are. This is all, of course, the blessing of God on what started as a frame-cutting operation in an Oklahoma garage.

I know a lot of this Hobby Lobby history may not feel like it applies to you, but stick with me and I promise I'll make it practical for you at the end.

When you have great wealth to manage, you will always have experts, financial managers, and advisors to help you with the task. This is as it should be because no one should make decisions about such vast sums alone. The traditional wisdom among financial advisors is that a man of my wealth should create a legacy for his children by setting up a complicated system of trusts and corporate structures to minimize estate taxes, which can often run as high as fifty-five percent. The goal, to put it crassly, is to beat the IRS so that you have more to pass on to your heirs.

So you create various trusts and legal structures that provide for the transference of wealth in a way that the tax code allows you to avoid as many taxes as possible. In our case, our children received stock in the company. The two who have children of their own—Mart and Steve—set up additional trusts to pass their wealth on to their children, our grandchildren. All of this was done, as it traditionally is, with an eye to lower the tax impact at the time of death.

It is not a process for the fainthearted. It involves mountains of paperwork and armies of lawyers. Hours of discussion lead to lengthy explanations by experts, which are turned into documents to sign not once but a dozen times! The hope is that when it is all done there is peace. You are supposed to live in the assurance that your wealth is as safe as it can be from the IRS and that everyone in your family is provided for in abundance for years to come.

Barbara and I did as we were advised. We hired smart people and told them to use the wisest instruments and strategies possible. We did all that is usually done to pass wealth on to children and grandchildren. In some cases, we ended up with costly insurance products. Part of my advice is to watch for those who have a conflict of interest in working with you.

In any case, with all the planning we'd done, we should have been at peace. We should have breathed a sigh of relief and then never again had to trouble ourselves with such matters.

It didn't happen that way.

The truth is that I grew more and more uneasy. Something about the whole process didn't seem right to me. Odd as it may sound, I was troubled in my spirit, in my innermost being. It wasn't just that I mentally objected to what was happening. It was that something seemed out of line with God's will.

I couldn't sleep.

I thought about the matter constantly and probably wore Barbara out talking about it.

The traditional approach to passing on wealth to the next generation separated my unified Christian family by breaking up or passing down ownership to children, grandchildren, and great-grandchildren. I envisioned a few generations down that we could have hundreds of shareholders each with their own interests. We were a family deeply committed to each other and to Christian purposes for the wealth we had been given. Yet the approach we had agreed to for transferring wealth broke up my family into individual pieces.

Under this traditional approach, it struck me that the aim was to promote the individual interests of hundreds of shareholders. Those shareholders could or would vote their interests instead of the larger family interests. That made me uncomfortable. It seemed to me that we needed to keep a united vision for our family. It doesn't matter if you're a wealthy business owner, a rookie entrepreneur, or a couple planning their family and the next five years, breaking up your family's vision is never a good thing.

The Importance of Family Vision

As I paced my office and went for long walks, I could see in my mind how this would play out over the generations. With each transfer of wealth from parents to children, the wealth and the vision would again subdivide. To me, subdivide just seemed like a fancy word for get weaker. We wouldn't be passing a unified whole down through the generations. We would be parceling out pieces over generations, and ultimately there would be nothing left.

I need to make clear that none of my concerns had to do with some moral inferiority on the part of my children or grandchildren. I trust them all entirely, and if they were the only factors involved, I would not have any concerns at all.

No, the problem I could see was not with my heirs, whom I love and have devoted myself to. It was with the traditional processes of wealth transfer. I saw these processes as the enemy of family vision and wealth creation through the generations.

I'm grateful to be able to speak of my trust in my children and grandchildren. We all regularly see headlines that confirm how wealth transferred to unprepared heirs can lead to disaster. The tabloids and gossip columns are full of stories about celebrity offspring who, as the saying goes, have more money than they know what to do with and, to be frank, repeatedly do stupid things with it. Even among those who try to follow in their parents' footsteps, the failure rate of family businesses being run by the second generation of family is a shocking seventy percent. By the time the third generation comes along, the rate goes up to eighty-five percent.[15]

It is almost enough to make us agree with Andrew Carnegie, the nineteenth-century steel magnate, who bluntly declared, "The almighty dollar bequeathed to a child is an almighty curse. No man has the right to handicap his son with such a burden as great wealth."[16]

Of course such sentiments and failures played in my mind as I considered these matters of legacy. Yet I knew that Barbara and I had raised a deeply Christian family, that our children had proven themselves time and again, and that wealth wouldn't turn them into the same kind of immoral spendthrifts we sometimes see in news stories.

Still, I was certain that this traditional approach to transferring wealth was wrong. I was disappointed with what had been set in place for my family. Something had to change.

Bill High, who helped me write this book, had some great advice at this point. Bill is a lawyer and an executive with The Signatry: A Global Christian Foundation. He first entered our lives as a financial advisor to Mart when the movie *Beyond the Gates of Splendor* was being made. Bill advised Mart about nonprofit law and offered numerous helpful solutions to challenges facing that project. This led to other roles for Bill in advising our family and company. His wisdom and easygoing manner made him perfectly suited for facilitating communication and creating consensus on many important matters.

At Mart's recommendation, I asked Bill to meet with our family. He did, and very gently offered his observations about what was in place and what might be done to facilitate the management trust. The family seemed to trust him immediately. They asked if he could help us get through this critical transition. Bill agreed. I was grateful.

What Is Guiding Your Family's Future?

Bill spoke of taking a complicated and legalistic succession plan and remaking it into a family legacy plan. He spoke of it as a kind of constitution that would guide the family for generations. It would provide a family vision, a family mission, guiding values, a giving statement, prerequisites for being a member of the management trust, and, finally, a wise plan for implementing all of this.

I found it easy to work with Bill. He enjoys fast-paced conversations like I do, and he often showed up for our meetings with notes written out on a napkin—just like me. Perhaps more important, he has a story similar to mine of growing up in poverty, and he cares deeply about family. A bit less important but still helpful is that we share a love of Oreo cookies. And Bill seems to enjoy my lawyer jokes. Most lawyers don't. My grandchildren say that "you know you're family when Grandpa gives you a hard time."

What followed was a yearlong process of creating and embracing a Green family legacy plan. It wasn't without thoughtful, sacrificial, and sometimes painful decision making. But we were committed.

We started with a series of family retreats. There were hours of discussion and exploring options. We even got into examining the personality types of each family member and learning about each other by using tools like StrengthsFinder. We wanted to understand how each person is wired. Ultimately, this led to the development of our mission, vision, and values statements.

Our goal was to protect the company through the generations and to define who would manage that trust and for what purposes. And we did. We completed and signed the Green Stewardship Trust. Into this trust went the entirety of the Green family wealth.

The very first page of our document creating this trust establishes its purposes:

1. To honor God with all that has been entrusted to us
2. To protect, preserve, and grow the value of the Green Family Companies
3. To use the assets of Green Family Companies to create, support, and leverage the efforts of Christian ministries

By the second page, the document spells out how company donations will be dispersed. Perhaps the most revolutionary part of this endeavor is that our operative documents now direct that if the trustees ever get the notion to sell or liquidate more than ten percent of the company, the rules for distribution are:

1. Ninety percent to Christian ministries
2. Ten percent to a special-needs fund for family members who encounter some kind of urgent situation, such as a life-threatening disease

Nothing will go into the pockets of a shareholder or a trustee. This means it will do trustees little good to sell the company for personal gain. By insisting on this, we hope to keep Hobby Lobby on track as God's company, not ours. We want it to continue for decades, perhaps even centuries, as an ongoing source of financial fuel for God's work around the world.

The analogy of the tree is the best way to explain what we were trying to do. We think of Hobby Lobby as a strong, fruitful tree. Every season it bears another crop of, say, apples. If we take care of the tree—cultivating the soil around it, making sure it gets adequate water, spraying it as needed—it will yield wonderful fruit.

Anyone in the family, or even outside the family, is welcome to help take care of the tree. If they work diligently, they can receive a share of the results. If you are a good janitor at Hobby Lobby, you will get a bag of apples. If you qualify to be a vice president, you receive a whole bushel basket of apples.

Yet understand this: You cannot have the tree. It will never belong to you. It belongs to someone else. This is what we were trying to achieve with the Green Stewardship Trust, and I'm proud of its uniqueness and the way it honors God. But this basic concept is for everyone. The tree—your wealth and resources—belongs to God. And if your vision and mission reflect this truth, the tree will act as a safeguard for generations to come.

Switching Over

This philosophy was a whole new way of thinking for the family. We had to absorb the mentality that what we held in our hands was not our asset but rather a stewardship responsibility. We needed to manage this company for God's purposes and glory. If we messed it up, he would no doubt take it away from our family and give it to others who would be more faithful with it. I'd seen too many examples of families who had started companies only to see them fail when ownership of the company or profit distributions became more important than the stewardship of the company.

It was unfortunate that we had already made estate-planning arrangements that gave each family member control of their own slice of the wealth. This meant that we had to engage in long conversations and planning sessions to create the new trust that would supersede and absorb all previous trusts. Everyone would have to sign off on canceling the old and installing the new.

We finally got to that place during a family weekend meeting in November 2011. All of G2 and G3 agreed with the new plan and were willing to put it in writing.

This legal document prevents Barbara and me as founders from getting our hands on the net worth of the company. The same holds true for our kids and grandkids. None of us can touch it. We can only earn a salary for our work.

To some observers, this is absolutely radical. I disagree. I would call it radical to say that we own Hobby Lobby and can do with it whatever we want. Sorry, but that's just not true. When we go to God's Word, we see that the accumulations of this life are not ours. "Every good and perfect gift is from above, coming down from the Father," says the New Testament writer James (1:17).

Safeguards

Now someone might object, "But rules can be revised. What is to say somebody won't change the arrangements once you and Barbara are gone?"

We carefully considered that very possibility.

The trust currently has five trustees: Barbara, our three children, and me. As the years go by, some of us will need to be replaced, of course, but the total number is capped at seven. Each new trustee must be of like mind.

Among other things:

1. The person must submit a written personal testimony of salvation through faith in Christ.
2. The person must then share this testimony verbally before the other trustees.
3. Each year, the person must read and sign the ten-point Green Family Statement of Faith. (See appendix.)

4. The person must affirm the Green Family Vision, Mission, and Values Statement.

This language confirms that we are doing everything we can to cement what Hobby Lobby is and why it exists in the minds and hearts of those who come after us.

On the Receiving End

I have come to see my role in business as dependent rather than independent. The book *Family. Money.* says it very well: "God's plan for our wealth acquisition is perhaps better described as wealth reception. Since he owns it, wealth is his to give, not ours to take or create."[17] If you want to refer to David Green as a "wealth receiver," that's fine with me. I try to approach every day with hands that are open, not grasping.

One of my heroes is a man I've mentioned already, missionary pioneer Bob Hoskins, who along with his son Rob has founded the outstanding ministry called OneHope. Bob tells about his early days of living in Beirut, Lebanon, when that city was a stable anchor point for all kinds of nonprofit organizations. In 1975, the Lebanese Civil War broke out and conditions deteriorated rapidly. The downtown area, previously an oasis for business and culture, became a no-man's land called the Green Line. Bob remembers the night the US embassy called to say they were evacuating all nonessential Americans as soon as possible.

"My family and I threw things into suitcases and headed out. I stood there at the apartment door with the key in my hand, taking one last look at all our furniture, our personal treasures, the special carvings I had received as gifts when I'd been preaching in various countries of Africa and Asia. I thought to myself, I wonder if I'll ever see any of this again."

The Hoskinses headed down the stairs, through the dark streets, and soon made their way to the nearby island nation of Cyprus. From there it was on to America for a number of months. Eventually, the Lebanese turmoil settled down enough for them to return. "We came back with our hearts in our throats that day, headed up the stairs, turned the key in the lock, opened the door . . . and sighed with relief. Everything was exactly as we had left it! Our prayers had been answered. We were home again."

A few years later, the clouds of war darkened over Beirut a second time. Bob Hoskins and his family watched nervously. Eventually, the call to evacuate came again. Once again the family was forced to pack up quickly and get out, leaving their apartment behind.

When the smoke of battle cleared, they returned as they had before, climbing the stairs, turning the key in the lock. This time, though, their home had been destroyed. Couches and beds lay broken, dishes were smashed, and irreplaceable souvenirs were demolished or missing. Their belongings were no more.

When Bob tells this story, he concludes with this dramatic statement: "Hold the things of this world very lightly. They may be there for you to enjoy tomorrow or they may not. The Bible says, 'We brought nothing into the world, and we can take nothing out of it.' Live with an open hand before God; it's the only way in a dangerous, unpredictable world."

I feel the same way about Hobby Lobby.

It's not mine to guard; it belongs to God. We happen to be headquartered in Oklahoma City, which is the heart of Tornado Alley. We've never been hit, but we certainly could be. Meanwhile, we've lost individual stores across the country, such as when a class four tornado (EF4) slammed us to splinters in Tuscaloosa, Alabama, in April 2011.

If the corporate offices and warehouses—nine million square

feet of space—all went flying across the prairie, I'm sure I would be dismayed. Ultimately, though, it's God's enterprise. He holds its future. My job is simply to make it as productive for his purposes as I can, for as long as he chooses to let it stand.

Here is the surprise. There's a certain peace in recognizing this. It actually relieves anxiety for me. I can sleep at night again. These assets are not mine to worry over. The one in charge will take care of them as he sees fit, and I only need to execute what he tells me to do.

You see, a legacy lovingly prepared and wisely transferred should lead to peace for everyone involved. Many people who hear of the unusual way that the Green family is passing its wealth through the generations think that the mechanics are the important part of the story.

No, the important part of the story is the pleasure of God and the peace of God that rests on our lives now that we have done his will. This kind of blessing is possible only when the glory of God is the goal of all we do.

We have a private family document that Bill helped us create. It outlines the vision, mission, and values of the Green family. In it, we clearly define wealth: "Wealth: defined as intellectual, social, financial, and spiritual capital."

So how are you managing your wealth? How do you plan to transfer it to your children and to their children? Can you imagine the blessing of God upon a family who stewards their wealth well?

The word economy gets passed around in the media so much I wonder if we really know what it means. It's used primarily to refer to how well our country is doing monetarily. But that's only one way to look at it. For me, a more helpful way to understand economy is the "careful management of resources." It implies the need for a steward—the person who does the careful management of resources.

In the Old Testament book of Proverbs, the final chapter describes what has become known as the Proverbs 31 Woman. If you read the chapter, you'll notice that the woman being described is a world-class economist.

She's a careful manager of all her resources: intellectual, social, financial, spiritual, even aesthetic. Her diligent work is connected to her spiritual fervor for God. She honors and reveres God, and her life expresses this through brilliant stewardship. We all can learn from this wonderful woman how to pursue the careful management of everything God has given us.

Part 5

THE ETERNAL LEGACY THAT IS RIGHT NOW

For if you remain silent at this time, relief and deliverance for the Jews will arise from another place, but you and your father's family will perish. And who knows but that you have come to royal position for such a time as this?

—The Book of Esther

Earthly goods are given to be used, not to be collected.

—Dietrich Bonhoeffer

One gives freely, yet grows all the richer; another withholds what he should give, and only suffers want. Whoever brings blessing will be enriched, and one who waters will himself be watered.

—The Teacher

Chapter 11

STAYING RICH

Do not lay up for yourselves treasures on earth, where moth and rust destroy and where thieves break in and steal, but lay up for yourselves treasures in heaven, where neither moth nor rust destroys and where thieves do not break in and steal.

—Jesus of Nazareth, Son of God

I REALIZE THAT RUNNING a billion dollar company doesn't exactly make me just one of the guys from a purely financial standpoint. Money tends to separate us in our culture, and that's unfortunate because I'm just like you. I get up every day, spend time with God, kiss my wife, eat some breakfast, and go to work.

I'm just a man. I started my career working retail, stocking shelves. I got married and started a family. I've lost sleep wondering about the future of my wife and kids. Now I'm entering that area of the baton exchange, and I want to do it well. I want us all to do it well. I want my grandchildren to grow up understanding that generosity begins with an attitude that extends into every aspect of life, not just money. I want them to understand that today begins *their* legacy. Because if there's one thing I've discovered, it's that true wealth encompasses all of life.

That's the big idea. I believe we can chart a course for our lives and our families that allows us to think beyond one generation. We can outline our vision, mission, and values. And we can live that out through our generosity. These ideas will allow us to stay rich for generations—not just in a monetary sense but in a values sense.

Some of you reading this book are standing in shoes similar to my own. You are nearing the end of your life, wondering how to finish well and leave a legacy that will bless your family and those they interact with for generations to come. Some of you are just starting out in life, taking your first steps toward those dreams and plans.

Whether you're at the end or the beginning of life, I want to challenge you to do three things:

1. Work with all your heart, for God and not for men.
2. Hold those plans lightly, because you really have no idea what the Lord has in store.
3. Consider now what you want your legacy to be. It is not too early to begin.

The decisions you make today will affect the legacy you leave behind. Whether you are a young business man who has found himself encountering what the world sees as success both in career and family life, or a young woman who recently graduated and has no idea what is in front of you, today is the right day to make your decisions in light of the truth that God owns it all. Live your life in this world while investing your wealth in the next.

Only One Life

When I was growing up, we did not have much artwork in our house. Money was tight, and our family got along with just the basics of life.

Knicknacks, frills, and family photos were not to be found in our simple home. But there was one plaque on the wall I have never forgotten. It was a short poem:

> Only one life
> 'Twill soon be past
> Only what's done
> For Christ will last.

In my teen years and for quite a few years into my adulthood, the words of that poem stirred up guilt inside me whenever I remembered them. Assuming that "what's done for Christ" meant work done as a pastor with his flock, as an evangelist on the street corner, or as a missionary to remote tribes in Africa, I felt defeated because I knew those were things I could not do. Not until my late thirties did I discover the joy of giving to God's work and come to realize its lasting value.

Until recently, I had no idea that those lines were actually part of a longer poem with a very interesting story. It was written by the son of a wealthy British family, Charles Thomas (C. T.) Studd, who lived from 1860 to 1931. His father had made a fortune producing indigo dye in India. Charles and his brothers attended the best schools England could offer, first Eaton and then Cambridge, where Charles became, as some have called him, the Michael Jordan of cricket. Charles represented his country on the national cricket team and became a household name in Britain. He knew that when he turned twenty-five years old, he would inherit a large sum—some $25 million in today's dollars—from his father's estate.

Yet by that time, God had touched his heart and called him to service overseas. He started out in China, where he married a young Irish woman of like mind. Together, they gave away their entire portion of the Studd fortune to such ministries as George Müller's orphanage, D. L. Moody's Bible school in Chicago, the China Inland Mission, and the Salvation Army. From that point on, they trusted God to supply their needs.

Ten years of work in China were followed by six years in India, where Studd's father had become rich. C.T.'s health was not the greatest by then, and neither was his wife's. After India, he pressed on for another twenty-one years in the heart of Africa until he died and was buried there at age seventy. His passion was to share the gospel with those who had never heard of Christ. And it's the gospel passion that oozes from his nine-stanza poem. Here are a couple of verses as examples.

> Two little lines I heard one day,
> Traveling along life's busy way;
> Bringing conviction to my heart,
> And from my mind would not depart;
> Only one life, 'twill soon be past,
> Only what's done for Christ will last.
>
> Give me, Father, a purpose deep
> In joy or sorrow Thy Word to keep;
> Faithful and true whate'er the strife,
> Pleasing Thee in my daily life;
> Only one life, 'twill soon be past
> Only what's done for Christ will last.

C. T. Studd was a man who did not let family money distract him from what was truly important in life. History tells us that his children caught his values system. Three of his daughters married Christian leaders. Some two thousand Congolese showed up for his funeral in July 1931.

I will never be the speaker and writer he was, but I am just as committed to the goals he exemplified. Of the various scriptures under the plexiglas on my desk, this is perhaps the most compelling in my heart and mind: "This and this only has been my appointed work: getting this news to those who have never heard of God, and explaining how it works by simple faith and plain truth" (1 Tim. 2:7–8 *The Message*).

I hope they put that verse on my tombstone. Through the efforts of the company God has allowed us to build, I want as many people as possible to come to know Christ as Savior. Fortunately, if God blesses the values and financial arrangements that I've described in this book, then there is no reason my work will not go on long after I'm gone.

I can think of nothing that would make me happier.

Eternal Riches

When we're young, sometimes we think there's a magic key in life that will answer all the questions or solve all the problems. It's easy to think that life possesses some big secret and that when we find success somehow we'll attain this key to unlock all the mysteries of life. But now, as part of the emeritus faculty of life, I can say that it's much simpler than that: be faithful with what God puts in front of you, and invest in the things of heaven.

Much of what I've said is summed up in the book of Matthew. Eugene Peterson, the pastor who wrote the Bible paraphrase *The Message*, puts it like this: "Don't hoard treasure down here where it gets eaten by moths and corroded by rust or—worse!—stolen by burglars. Stockpile treasure in heaven, where it's safe from moth and rust and burglars. It's obvious, isn't it? The place where your treasure is, is the place you will most want to be, and end up being" (Matt. 6:19–21 *The Message*).

How do you stockpile treasure in heaven?

First, stockpiling treasure is a heart issue. If I value the things of this world and what those things do for me in the here and now, then my heart's allegiance and love is plain to see.

But if the unseen things of this world hold a deeper value—things like love, grace, service, humility, and faith—then it reveals the size of my soul. I want to be remembered more for the size of my soul than for the size of my bank account. I want G2 and G3 to identify themselves by the depth of their faith in Jesus Christ, the expanse of their love, and the richness of their grace. I want their souls to be big for the work of God's kingdom.

The second thing needed to stockpile treasure is a heavenly perspective. That means doing my best to look at the world the way God sees it. This is hard, especially in our very loud digital world. It's difficult to cut through the noise and really see the world with eternal eyes. I have a heavenly perspective when I stop viewing relationships and everyday living as transactions that must happen. Our everyday should be an expression of worship toward the Creator.

This perspective doesn't just show up at our door. We must cultivate it, care for it. This is not a hermit lifestyle I'm talking about. Rather, it's an engaged lifestyle in which you and I work hard at our jobs and marriages and families to glorify our Creator.

When we live with our hearts bent in, listening to God, and if we live with a heavenly perspective, then we'll grab hold of eternal things. Things that will never fade. That's what I want my resources, time, and money to work toward: building things that last forever.

Chapter 12

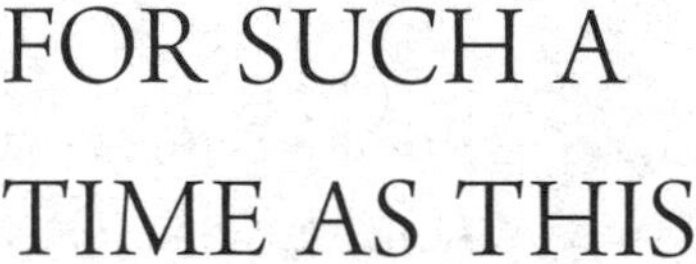

FOR SUCH A TIME AS THIS

Everybody wants to enjoy heaven after they die, but they don't want to be heavenly-minded while they live.

—D. L. Moody, Evangelist

This is my call to action: we need a sense of urgency about God's priorities for the resources we've been given.

I began this book by talking about pursuing the big ideas that made our country great: valuing our heritage, our unseen legacy, family, the idea that wealth is more than money. Each of these ideas reflects Jesus. He showed us a true generous spirit during his three-year ministry, especially his final hours on this earth. When I mention pursuing these big ideas, I'm referring to having a soul and a perspective that mirror our Lord's.

Next, we discussed how our generosity leaves a legacy, one that's seen and unseen. A seen legacy looks like those things we manage in this world, like our money and physical resources or assets. An unseen legacy, however, possesses so much more power because it stirs within our hearts and minds. It's our character, values, and beliefs. I say unseen because it begins inside of us, but the fruit of the unseen legacy is anything but invisible. It is a living, breathing human being living their life for Jesus, using everything they've been given—their money, time, and resources—for his glory.

This generosity shows us that if we give everything away, we'll get it all back again in ways we can't imagine. Those ways might be tangible, such as financially, but more important, they are also intangible ways. Like the joy that comes from giving, the satisfaction of our everyday work, and the rule of peace in our lives because we've given our business, our families, and our vocations to God. This perspective, however, is counter-cultural in today's world.

Our culture today has deteriorated. That's because we've gotten so far away from God's Word. God's Word takes us away from ourselves. Our culture, on the other hand, points us toward ourselves.

What culture without God leads us to loving others?

Only God's Word does this.

It directs us toward others and their well-being. God's love for us compels us to love others. Imagine what that understanding does for a person, and then another, and then a culture.

This is why I believe it's so important for our family to commit our selves to the eternal things: man's soul and God's Word. These things are eternal.

But, as a culture, when you look at where our collective treasures lie, it reveals our heart. And that can look rather ugly—like greediness or self-centeredness. Our culture does not include the eternal things. What's important? Money and things immediately obtained that give us pleasure. But that stuff doesn't last.

With this eternal perspective firmly in mind, I want to leave you with three thoughts.

1. Don't Hope in Wealth, Hope in God

The chances that my great-great-great-grandchildren will know my name are slim to none. Hobby Lobby will not last forever. The hard-hitting reality is that there are only two things that will last—God's Word and people's souls.

Through the years I've led Hobby Lobby, I've tried to think about what it would look like for me to invest this company in what is dear to God's heart. I've tried to stay mindful of Jesus' warning: "For where your treasure is, there your heart will be also" (Matt. 6:21).

People have said to me, "Why do you continue to expand Hobby Lobby? Don't you have enough?" They look at our opening a new store every two weeks or they speculate about our profitability and they think we could afford to go on autopilot.

Our ongoing growth has nothing to do with increasing my personal income. For the last eleven years, I have taken home the same amount of salary even though company earnings have been rising strongly for decades. If I am still here eleven years from now, I will still be earning the same, though the business likely will demand more of me by then. Things will get harder and more complex if we grow to, say, $5 billion a year instead of today's $4 billion.

This is not about Barbara and me. This is not about setting up G2 or G3 for a plush future. This is not about dominating the arts-and-crafts industry. This is not about pushing out competitors. This is not about staying on the Forbes 400 list.

Then what is the point of our wealth?

There's a paragraph of scripture that is pretty straightforward for someone like me. Though the paragraph comes from a letter Paul wrote to Timothy a couple of thousand years ago, I think his words perfectly capture what should be our approach to wealth today.

> Command those who are rich in this present world not to be arrogant nor to put their hope in wealth, which is so uncertain, but to put their hope in God, who richly provides us with everything for our enjoyment.
>
> Command them to do good, to be rich in good deeds, and to be generous and willing to share.
>
> In this way they will lay up treasure for themselves as a firm foundation for the coming age, so that they may take hold of the life that is truly life.
>
> —1 Timothy 6:17–19

God's view of the purpose of wealth is to advance the things he cares about. He is far more interested in people around the world coming to know and love him than he is in whether the Green family members in Oklahoma City have an easy lifestyle. Whatever we can do to align with his goals is going to bring his smile.

So when we look at Hobby Lobby's bottom line, we see it in terms of the fun we're going to have helping ministries and organizations share the gospel of Jesus Christ. Yes, fun—that's the correct word.

We think about volunteers knocking on millions of doors in 150 nations offering a free booklet of truth—a booklet that we paid for.

We imagine schoolchildren in Bolivia or Uganda receiving a small *Book of Hope* keyed to their age level.

We think about people in the United States opening up their newspapers on Christmas or Easter and seeing our full-page ad about the Savior who came, died for them, and rose again.

These are the things that get us fired up.

Does God care whether our stores sell more posterboard, silk flowers, or wicker baskets? If the result of those sales is more people receiving the gospel, you bet he does. Dollars become ministry.

Perspective makes all the difference here. I like the way these authors put it:

> At some point in eternity-future, we must give an account of our handling of things. Family money is one of the things we must steward, or manage. It's not simply a matter of getting ours and meeting our needs.
>
> First and foremost, we are agents assigned to accomplish God's purposes; and we're given a portion from his wallet to do it.[18]

You hadn't exactly thought of God as having a wallet? Well, I know it's an unusual word picture, but it's a valid one. He is wealthier, you know, than you and me and Bill Gates and Warren Buffett all together. He just happens to have chosen to delegate a small part of his holdings to us.

2. Remember Your Position of Privilege

This is a critical time in the history of the world. Problems around the globe are getting worse each day. International conflicts are growing, with few solutions in sight. Young people are becoming more disillusioned about their future.

It's almost like the moment in history centuries ago when the superpower of the day, Persia, was about to wipe out the Jewish people. A man named Mordecai sent a message to his young cousin Esther, who had surprisingly risen to become queen: "If you remain silent at this time, relief and deliverance for the Jews will arise from another place, but you and your father's family will perish. And who knows but that you have come to royal position for such a time as this?" (Est. 4:14).

Esther rose to the challenge. It was dangerous. She was relatively new in the palace and didn't have that much clout with the king. Yet she ended up preventing an awful genocide.

Randy Alcorn has written wisely about the story of Esther:

> Just as Esther was in a position of privilege, so is nearly everyone reading this book. Are you educated and literate? Do you have food, clothing, shelter, a car, perhaps some electronic equipment? Then you are among the privileged, the world's wealthy.
>
> Why has God entrusted you with the privilege of wealth? For such a time as this. God has sovereignly raised you up.[19]

It's tough to picture yourself in a position of power such as Esther. As a culture, we've become so focused on ourselves that we don't pause, step back, and take in the bigger picture. But it's so important that we, as Christians, step back and assess our communities, our nation, and the world.

Our nation faces unprecedented times in terms of leadership. Never have we been so divided politically. Likewise, our churches stand divided on social issues, and much of the division stems from a lack of unity on the orthodox teachings of the Word of God. Whenever division raises its ugly head, you can bet that the religion of self has taken center stage.

But even as this time in which we live faces unprecedented divisions between progressive, liberal, and conservative Christians, and social breakdowns in the case of family and sexual ethics, the Christian community stands poised for dramatic influence. Christians, stewarding their gifts and talents well, are influencing our culture across many channels of influence. From Hollywood to education reform to social entrepreneurship, Christians are seizing the opportunity to effect change in their communities and country.

3. Life Is Like Crazy Eights

I hope you don't think this sounds too religious or fanciful. I'm dead serious in my belief that my responsibility to handle Hobby Lobby's assets is directly tied to God's endeavors in the world. He has asked folks like you and me to be on his team, to think like he thinks about resources, and to advance his priorities. I've been glad to say, "Count me in."

One author I read said that too many people think life is basically an oversized game of Monopoly, where the way to win is to accumulate as many properties as you can, either by purchasing outright or by clever trading with your opponents. Then you keep adding houses and hotels, extracting rent from the others, until you eventually drive them into bankruptcy. You sit back, rub your hands together, and start counting your stacks of cash.[20]

No, life is more like Uno or Crazy Eights, where the point is to run out of cards first. You want to deploy every card you have, knowing that each card left in your hand at the end counts against you. Don't get stuck at the time of your funeral with leftover cards![21]

The Bible passage I quoted earlier describes "lay[ing] up treasure… as a firm foundation for the coming age." Talk about a long-range investment strategy! We shouldn't add up the score of our business acumen until we get the report from eternity. Only then will we know how well we've done in life. To put it in a catchphrase, "You can't take it with you—but you can send it on ahead."[22]

That's what Barbara and I are determined to do. We think that's the purpose of the funds God has entrusted to us.

We have a responsibility to instill this mindset in the next generation. God has a lot to say in scripture about families making sure their values keep going down the line. Early in human history, as Noah's family emerged from the ark, "God said to Noah and to his sons with him: 'I now establish my covenant with you and with your descendants after you. . . . Never again will all life be destroyed by the waters of a flood'" (Gen. 9:8–9, 11). God unveiled a dazzling rainbow at that moment to seal his promise for all time.

The view is similar when he spoke to Abraham.

> I will establish my covenant as an everlasting covenant between me and you and your descendants after you for the generations to come, to be your God and the God of your descendants after you. The whole land of Canaan, where you now reside as a foreigner, I will give as an everlasting possession to you and your descendants after you; and I will be their God.
>
> Then God said to Abraham, "As for you, you must keep my covenant, you and your descendants after you for the generations to come."
>
> —Genesis 17:7–9

Clearly, the gift of "the whole land of Canaan"—a major stretch of real estate—was not just a God-and-Abraham deal. It was an asset for future generations to receive with understanding and gratitude, knowing that they were expected to play an important role in preserving it. The rest of the Old Testament story reveals how Abraham's descendants followed through with their calling.

When King David got the idea to expend a large amount of wealth for building a permanent home—a temple—for God in Jerusalem, God sent him a prophet named Nathan. He affirmed David's intent but declared that David's son would lead the construction project instead. The prophet's closing sentence was this: "Your house and your kingdom will endure forever before me; your throne will be established forever" (2 Sam. 7:16). Again, we see God's priority of a long-term view.

No wonder one of the most familiar psalms from this era ends with this exclamation: "For the Lord is good and his love endures forever; his faithfulness continues through all generations" (Ps. 100:5).

I hope that can be said of the Green family a hundred or two hundred years from now (if the Lord doesn't return first)—that God's faithfulness has been allowed to flourish through all our generations. I'm determined to do whatever I can while I'm here to set that expectation in place.

Accordingly, I've expanded my personal goals for life from the three I mentioned before to five. I've also changed the sequence.

The list now reads:

1. To have a great marriage
2. To raise children who are serving God
3. To be successful in business
4. To see our grandchildren and even our great-grandchildren serve God
5. To use our resources to tell as many people about Christ as we can

If all that comes to pass, I can die a happy man. I can stand before God at the final review and look forward to good news. Not that I've done everything perfectly; I certainly have not. Still, I will have concentrated on the things that I believe matter most to God: fulfilling his purposes and desires for a world in need.

EPILOGUE

WHY DID I WRITE THIS BOOK?

I didn't want to write it. I'm an introvert, and I don't really like crowds or attention. But a funny thing happened along the way.

From time to time, Bill and I host generosity gatherings at my office in Oklahoma City. These gatherings feature top leaders from top businesses all across the country. Our focus during these times is to do nothing more than share our mutual stories around the themes of legacy and generosity.

These are simple gatherings: nothing more than fifteen to twenty people at a time. We meet for about one day. I share some of my journey, and we interact around each other's stories. At the end of the time, we ask people very plainly how their thinking and their actions might change on these subjects.

My hope in these gatherings is pretty simple. I hope that people will respond to God's prompting in their lives. I'm quick to point out in these gatherings that my story is still a work in progress. I don't have it all figured out. And what I've done with my family is not what everyone should do. We are just one family.

We've had some amazing responses. Here's a sampling from a recent session:

- "I am now very focused on becoming a better steward, not just of money and time, but of *all* of life, including things that wouldn't normally process as things to be stewarded . . . my wife, my kids, my 'power,' pain, love—certainly money, business, and time. The idea that I don't 'own' anything . . . it makes me a steward—so now I will not be someone that can be angry or 'hurt' when it is removed . . . I am thankful for this 'insight' . . . it's been fun, but also difficult, to work on."

- "Profound. Talking many next steps with my wife. Challenged. The team at my company is also clamoring for a debrief. Thank you."
- "Since the event, I have been relying on God even more and waiting on God to move. Also, I liked the way David approached faith by sharing what's important to him."
- "The concept of ownership and equity was pretty mindblowing for me. It greatly changes my thought process as I move forward in my own life."
- "The key takeaway from the event was the wisdom imparted by both David Green and the other business leaders during the session. Hearing stories of how they have seen God working in their lives and in their business was inspiring and provides a 'spurring on' and challenge."

Some people take action. I've seen some leaders take steps to begin giving away their business. I've seen others just make a pledge to increase their giving. Some take bold steps of faith in their businesses. Some just need to acknowledge that God is in fact the owner of everything they have.

I'm encouraged most of all by those who take action with respect to their families. There are those with young children who begin to think longer term. How can they impact five generations of their family? Some take steps to engage their children in giving. I encourage them to set their compass by drawing up a vision statement, a mission statement, and a values statement that can guide their families for generations.

As we hosted these gatherings, people asked us to write down the story. The first request was for the technical side of things—how we arranged the estate, how we arranged the estate documents, and issues of succession. But we found people were also wrestling with the nontechnical ideas of wealth transfer.

That's why we have this book: because people kept asking for it. And because Bill kept pushing me to write it. In fact, he was kind of annoying about it.

Our hope—mine and Bill's—is that like the people who come to these gatherings, you might be inspired by what you've read. But our hope is that you'll take action as well.

These are really basic ideas:

- We are not owners of anything. God owns everything.
- God wants us to be good stewards of everything he's put into our hands.
- We all have wealth—our intellectual capital, our social capital, our emotional capital, our spiritual capital, and our financial capital.
- Stewardship produces responsibility: as stewards, we need to be found faithful.
- The great joy of stewardship is generosity: giving it away because we get it all back again in the form of joy.

Our job as wise stewards is to pass on that wealth—all forms of it—to future generations. Passing on financial wealth is the easiest form of capital to pass on, yet in most cases it should be the last form of capital to pass on because of its inherent danger.

I know that many reading this book will not consider themselves to be financially wealthy, which is fine. This book is for everyone. We are all stewards. We are all stewards of the story that God has given us. It is a good story. There are elements of pain and great joy. But it is our story. It is a story of redemption and hope.

Let me speak as a father, a grandfather even, to those reading. Our call in this day and age is to preserve and to pass on our story—our legacy—to those coming after us. Our children. Our grandchildren. Our great-grandchildren. Even those children we will never know or see.

Psalm 78:5–6 says:

> He decreed statutes for Jacob
>   and established the law in Israel,
> which he commanded our ancestors
>   to teach their children,
> so the next generation would know them,
>   even the children yet to be born,
>   and they in turn would tell their children.

I think that is what God intended all along, that one generation will tell the next, and they in turn will tell the next. It was to be an ongoing story. Here's our clarion call: if we recover this idea—if we give our lives to this idea of passing wealth on to future generations—then we'll get it all back again in the form of future generations who will still follow hard after Christ.

Perhaps it is in such a time as this that God is calling men, women, and children to live this way—to live for ideas bigger than themselves and to invest in things bigger than themselves. And if we do, we will bring lasting change and hope to our world.

READER'S GUIDE

I HOPE READING THIS BOOK raised questions in your mind. Maybe you and your spouse grabbed this book and went through it together. Or perhaps your small group went through it. I love the idea of God's family learning and asking questions together.

So, by all means, share this book and its ideas with friends and family. Even if they don't read the book, talk to them about what you're thinking and learning. You never know what a simple conversation might do for someone, even yourself.

My prayer is that the book works as an igniter of ideas, questions, and actions. And to facilitate this, we (Bill and I) put together this reader's companion. Here's how it works. We first summarize the main idea from the chapter. We then provide two sections that encourage you (and your friends or family) to reflect, and then provide some ideas for further discussion. Naturally, they're labeled "Reflection" and "Discussion."

What is reflection? All it really means is that you take time out of your day to think about it further. I would even encourage you to pray about it. Ask yourself, "What is the main idea? How does it apply to me? What is its significance in my life? How will this idea affect culture?"

Then there's discussion. And don't think you need to use these questions verbatim. We include them here as helps, guides, starters. No doubt you have your own questions. If so, by all means, use them. But even so, we've provided some questions with each chapter. And remember, good reflection equals good discussion. Don't shortchange yourself. Do the time, think, then discuss.

Okay, time to get to it.

An Overview

Here's an interesting thought: write a letter from your eighty-year-old self. What will you write? What will you say to yourself about how to live a meaningful life?

Let's face it, at eighty years of age, you are looking in the rearview mirror more than you are looking forward.

The questions really are different at this stage of life. And at age eighty, we face certain realities. Quite likely, our possessions shine less brightly. On the other hand, the things that give us great joy are the intangibles:

- A phone call from a friend
- The touch of your spouse's hand on yours
- A quiet walk observing God's creation
- The presence of your children
- The laughter of your grandchildren

These are the things that matter. It matters that your children still want to talk to you, that they share your values, and that they are succeeding in a similar way with their children.

Chapter 1: What I've Learned That's Most Important

In chapter 1, I introduced the idea that we've lost sight of some of the big ideas in our country, like recognizing the people who have gone before us and planted seeds in our lives, that wealth is more than money, and that part of our legacy is the joy of giving. Often the big ideas are challenged in the heat of the moment, much like our family had to experience with the United States Supreme Court case. And yet it's during testing like that that your values rise to the top.

As we look to the future of our country, and in a more narrow sense as we look to the future of our individual families, we can return to these big ideas. I focus on them here as a way to at least raise the question of how we think about family. If we recapture the big ideas, then we can achieve legacies that last beyond one generation.

Reflection

1. Have you had a time of trial like our family experienced? Was it a time of peace for you? Or was it a time of anxiety? Consider Matthew 6:25–33 and how you might apply these verses as a family.
2. As you reflect on your past and our country's history, what do you see as the big ideas that have been timeless?
3. What is your view of today's times? Are we at one of the greatest times in the history of the world? What are you thankful for?

Discussion

1. In this chapter, I've suggested that we must think differently about how we pass on values and not just valuables. What kind of thinking must that be?
2. As you consider your own family, discuss how you've worked to pass on the value of giving and the value of work.
3. Read John 17. These words reflect some of the values that Jesus was passing on to his disciples. What themes do you see there?

Chapter 2: Shared Vision

I believe that together we can really turn our country around, but only if we begin, as individuals, by considering how our actions affect future generations. From there, I believe we must work together with a shared vision toward a brighter future. To accomplish this, you and I must model passing a lasting legacy to the next generation.

To me, this is exciting, but also very serious. Passing the baton, as I discussed, takes careful consideration and awareness. But the rewards can (and will) be extraordinary. Think about the relay team once again. It's easy to forget, in talking about passing the baton, how important the element of team or, in our case, community is. You and I must think not just in terms of ourselves but in terms of how our actions affect those around us.

Reflection

1. How well do you believe people understand the value and the idea of passing the baton, or the generational handoff? How well do you? Have you considered how important the element of community or team is when considering legacy?
2. In my family, the phrase "only what's done for Christ will last" became the compass setting for my life. As you consider your past, what lessons from your parents, teachers, or friends became key for your future direction?
3. Write out your own definition of legacy. Does it differ from how we are discussing it in this book? Or maybe you've yet to consider legacy. In that case, write down a definition you will remember, and then jot down some ideas on how you can consistently think about legacy in more ways than just money.

Discussion

1. Often when we talk about blessings, we consider them in the here and now—what's immediately in front of us. But C. T. Studd encourages us to think about the idea that "what's done for eternity will last." How might that mindset affect how we run our lives?
2. How many people do you know who are like me—people who had modest goals but saw their life's work become far more than they ever imagined? What caused their "success"? Was it a grand plan of their own? Consider Deuteronomy 8:18.
3. "You will be judged by how well the generation behind you did after you were gone." Do you agree or disagree? Why?

Chapter 3: The Invisible Legacy

You can't always see legacy. I know this might sound or feel different to some, but there is so much more to legacy, and wealth, for that matter, than meets the eye. The characteristics my family passed to me are priceless. They molded me into the man I am today. Characteristics such as perseverance, loyalty, and grace are just a few examples of the invisible legacy.

Sure, wealth can be an accumulation of money. But wealth also takes the form of resources, ideas, knowledge, wisdom, and so on. When you and I learn to identify legacy and wealth as more than money, our world opens up. We find that we have so much to steward, to care for.

I'm interested in leaving a legacy that transcends money. In doing so, I hope to instill in my family the characteristics that will govern, steward, and care for the world around them, starting with their own families and communities.

Reflection

1. As you consider your family story, write down your best memories. The most painful memories. What lessons were learned from both?
2. Have you ever thought about your own legacy? If you have, how do you think about it? Do you see it as affecting more than your immediate family?
3. Maybe the legacy left to you isn't so great. That's okay. Identify the things in the legacy left to you that you want to omit or correct. Write down how you want to correct the invisible legacy in your life. That's a hard thing to do because it will demand vulnerability. But getting beyond hurts or letdowns can do wonders for the building up of hope in our lives.

Discussion

1. If you're comfortable, discuss question 3 from the Reflection section with your small group or spouse, friend or coworker. I know this might be hard, but I think it might be helpful to discuss the roadblocks to developing a lasting legacy.
2. What are your fears associated with leaving a legacy? How might these fears hinder you from passing the baton well?
3. Read Psalm 74:4–8. Discuss how one generation can practically communicate its ideas and values to subsequent generations.

Chapter 4: The Rule of Peace

It took a national event to remind me that God has everything in his hand. Our battle with the SCOTUS and our subsequent win did so much for my faith. But most of all, it reminded me that Hobby Lobby, and all that I put my hands to and all my resources and possessions, is God's. This is so freeing!

When we cling to our possessions or even our work and the status that goes along with it, it can corrupt us, even ruin us. It can also be an obstacle for real growth in our lives. We like to feel in control of things. "I got this!" we say. But we don't have it. God does. When we realize this, it makes the tough decisions a bit easier, and it clears out anxiety and replaces it with a peace beyond our understanding.

Reflection

1. I think trusting God can be measured by how much control we're willing to give up. When you trust someone, there's a willingness attached to it. You'll let go. How easy or hard is it for you to trust God?
2. If your family had to come together for a major decision, including different generations, how aligned do you think they would be?
3. Consider instances or events in your life when your back was up against the wall and you needed rescue. What did you learn from those moments?

Discussion

1. How do you balance the idea of submitting to government (Rom. 13:7) with the idea of standing for your beliefs contrary to government law (Daniel 6)?

2. How has trust eroded in our society? Give examples of how you see this playing out.
3. Peace is a word we associate with war. It serves as its opposite. What is at war in your life that keeps you from peace? It could be two things vying for prominence. It could be doubt or the fear of letting go. What does it take to achieve peace in our lives spiritually, financially, and relationally?

Chapter 5: A Company Owned by God

I decided that Hobby Lobby was not mine but God's. In fact, I decided this about everything I put my hands to and all the things I possess in this world. When I made this decision, it relieved me of the burden of indecision and anxiety.

"Am I doing the right thing for the company? Are we going to make it?"

These questions vanished in the light of my new perspective.

Once I made that decision, I had to show that it made a difference in my life and work. In chapter 5 I showed you how we do business at Hobby Lobby. We believe that our faith convictions should guide how we live and work. If I say that God rules my life, then my actions should back up this claim. The same is true for my business.

Have you thought about how your faith manifests in your daily life—your family and work or school? I have, and I really try to do my best to live what I say. Or, as they say, to "walk the talk."

Reflection

1. Have you decided that God is king of your life? If so, how does your life look to those who are watching you? Do they

see a child of the king, or do they see just another Joe or Jane going about their business the same as everyone else?

2. In the book of Colossians, the writer, Paul the apostle, talks about the supremacy of Jesus Christ. If you've decided to follow Jesus, to be a child of the king, then Jesus should be your supreme guide. How does this bear out in your life? Is Jesus supreme, or are you? How does trust play into being a child of the king and submitting to the rule of Christ in our lives?
3. List your possessions—your car, your house, your clothes—and, if you have it, other real estate or ownership in a business. How tightly or loosely do you hold these items? Have you given over to God title to these items, and if not, what items should you be willing to let go?

Discussion

1. It is perhaps easier to say that God owns everything than it is to live it out. If God owns everything that you have, what should be practical evidence that you have lived out that notion?
2. Psalm 24:1 says that "the earth is the Lord's and everything in it." What are the ramifications of God's being the owner of everything? How does it affect our stewardship?
3. What is your most prized possession? Why? What would it mean to you to give it away?

Chapter 6: Journey into Generosity

In chapter 6 I shared a passage from Randy Alcorn's brilliant little book *The Treasure Principle*. It's helpful for me because it reminds me of the perspective I'm to have in this world. I want to include it here again, so you don't have to thumb back to chapter 6 to read it.

Imagine you're alive at the end of the Civil War. You're living in the South, but you are a Northerner. You plan to move home as soon as the war is over.

While in the South, you've accumulated lots of Confederate currency. Now, suppose you know for a fact that the North is going to win the war and the end is imminent. What will you do with your Confederate money?

If you're smart, there's only one answer. You should immediately cash in your Confederate currency for U.S. currency—the only money that will have value once the war is over. Keep only enough Confederate currency to meet your short-term needs.

As you reflect on Randy's passage, consider how generosity and trust go hand in hand.

Reflection

1. Randy challenges us to think with an eternal mindset. Our possessions will fade. What matters is how we use what we've been entrusted for God's kingdom. What perspective rules you? Are you going after the success of the world, or something else that's much greater? Are you clinging too tightly to your possessions? How does an eternal perspective affect how you use your time, money, and resources?
2. Second Corinthians 10:5 says that we must all stand before the judgment seat of Christ "so that each of us may receive what is due us for the things done in the body, whether good or bad." What do you think about standing at the judgment seat of Christ and being accountable for your stewardship?
3. My mother and father gave out of their big souls, not out of their monetary wealth. Their wealth was of a different

kind. Consider your own wealth—your God-given abilities, your work ethic, your love for others. How are you giving it all away? Why is it important that we be generous with our wealth?

Discussion

1. Read Randy Alcorn's passage out loud in your group or with your friend or loved one. Why is an eternal perspective important in a world in which the immediate rules the day? Can you think of other ways an eternal perspective can alter how you steward your wealth?
2. Go around and share your own journey with regard to generosity, giving, and stewarding. What circumstances led you to your approach to wealth? Who has influenced you the most in this area? Why?
3. I shared a story about writing a few checks to an organization with money I didn't have yet. I thought I couldn't afford to give the amount of money that God laid on my heart. What did this story mean to you? How did it affect your faith journey? Can you relate to it? Was there a time when you knew that God wanted you to do something very hard and with extreme faith? Did you go through with it, or did you end up regretting not doing it?

Chapter 7: The Joy of Giving

In chapter 7 I talked about the life-giving nature of joy. When we give of our wealth, as I defined it early on, joy follows. And by joy, I don't mean a temporary happiness. I'm talking about a joy that transcends our everyday expectations and desire for happiness.

There's a joy that comes from giving out of nothing, like my mother did. And I think this has more to do with trust in and love for God than anything. It's so easy in our culture to live lives homed in on our stuff, our schedules, our career paths, our ambition. I'm not saying that stuff is bad, but it shouldn't creep into our relationship with God. Rather, our relationship with God should guide those efforts. And that should bring us joy. Joy knowing he's in charge. Joy trusting his hand to provide for our every need.

Jesus said he came to this earth so that we can experience abundant life—that's life *through* him! He's the light of our life, the flame that ignites our everyday. When he is our light, our possessions change color or shape, so to speak. They look more like kingdom resources than personal possessions, and we're free to steward and give them according to God's pleasure. What joy!

Reflection

1. Think on the things in this life that bring the most joy. Describe why they do.
2. We often associate joy with a certain kind of happiness, like it's happiness at another level. Why do you think joy is unique, different from happiness altogether?
3. Giving is paradoxical. It would seem that the more we get for ourselves, the happier we would be, but it is actually the opposite—giving brings us joy. Why does this paradox exist?

Discussion

1. Go around the room and let everyone describe what it would take to develop the mindset from Matthew 13:44–46 that heaven is our joy. What seems to be the common denominator of joy in our lives?

2. What do you think it would take for giving in our society to go up from the current two percent of income to four percent, even six percent or more? What impact do you think that kind of giving would have around the world, and on the lives of the givers?
3. Talk with your group about the legacy of joy and generosity. We don't often talk of leaving a legacy like that. How can such a legacy have more of an impact than leaving behind a thriving business or loads of cash?

Chapter 8: The Nuts and Bolts of Generosity

Great, you're into generosity and leaving it as a legacy. Now what? In chapter 8 I gave some practical notes on giving. It starts with your church, then extends out. Find an organization you trust and resonate with, and dig in. Concentrate your resources there.

But first set some criteria for giving. Local versus global. Christian versus non. You and I are not the same, so we're going to have different criteria. That's okay. The fact that you're setting criteria is the important first step.

Next, we emphasized setting a giving amount, followed by the notion of setting a fire for the future. That means putting your resources toward something that will have future value, that will shape the future for the good. Some of the tips I gave work for individuals and families as well as businesses. Others are more specific to business owners. In any case, the point is to have a vision for your generosity.

Reflection

1. Do you have a vision for your generosity? Consider where and to whom you give. Are you spreading a little bit of money in

several directions? Might it make more sense to consolidate your efforts? What are the benefits of doing so?

2. Have you developed criteria for giving to organizations? If so, great! If not, write them out. I find that having a written guide helps a ton.
3. Do you have a family stewardship philosophy and an overall giving plan? If not, what would that plan include?

Discussion

1. Let's take a different approach for this discussion time. First, share your criteria for giving, or encourage one another with a good story about your own giving. Don't share amounts, unless you're comfortable doing so. Rather, just share how establishing a vision for giving helped you and inspired your giving.
2. What if you and your group or friends and family went in together on a giving project? What could you give in addition to money? How fun would it be to share this experience with folks you love and trust—to experience how giving can bring people together, especially when it's around a project everyone loves?
3. Discuss how you are giving as a family. What are some practical ways you can teach your children or grandchildren to give?

Chapter 9: The Legacy of Work

You might recall that I went a little old-school in chapter 9. Well, I am old-school, so I guess it's okay that folks might say that about me. I take it as a compliment. I believe our culture can learn a lot from the old-school. One of those things is the value of hard work, or the absence of an entitlement mindset. When we think we're entitled to certain things, long-lasting values are the first things to be affected.

I believe in finding your "whatever." Whatever it is that your hands find to do, do it to the glory of God. That could be digging a ditch or giving a sermon or mowing the grass or selling stocks on Wall Street. It doesn't matter what it is, *whatever* it is, do it with everything you have. And do it to bring God glory.

There's something about earning your way, being a good steward of what you've been entrusted with, and developing your character that never goes out of style. So, in that sense, old-school is, in my opinion, the best school!

Reflection

1. Consider the power of work in your life and in the greater culture. What does it produce in a person? How does it shape a person? Why is it so important to a thriving society?
2. Evaluate your community and the greater culture. What do you see, with regard to a good work ethic, that is positive, and what do you see that is negative? Sometimes we can go to extremes. Some people want to skate through life without really lifting a finger. Others become workaholics in pursuit of the almighty dollar. Where do you fall on this spectrum?
3. Do you know people who struggle with finding their calling? What do you think causes that struggle?

Discussion

1. Think about the state of work in our country. What has work become and where is it headed? Do we view work simply as a means to a paycheck, a means to providing us with leisure, luxury, and things we don't need?

2. What do you think of the concept from Ecclesiastes 9:10: "whatever your hand finds to do and doing it with all your might"? Do you think that you should determine your course of action in work, or does it happen more by being faithful in what you do and allowing God to show you the next step?
3. How can a sense of value be reinfused into the way in which we view work?

Chapter 10: The Art of the Generational Handoff

The concept of the generational handoff is so important. I think too many folks get it wrong or, even worse, don't think about it. This saddens me. I believe we each have a responsibility to the next generation—our families—not only to live well but to leave well.

But passing on a lasting legacy to the next generation doesn't just happen. You and I need to be proactive and thoughtful or else entropy will take over and things will crumble.

I love having a vision for our family's legacy. We have gone out of our way to make sure a vision and a plan are in place. That vision is guided by a set of principles. It's our measuring stick for generosity and our guide for legacy. It helps us know who we are, where we've come from, and where we're going. In all of that, God is at the center.

Without a plan and a vision, the company my wife and I have built from humble beginnings in our garage, and the family we've been blessed to have could easily be at risk for destruction—financial and moral. I've seen too many wealthy people squander their opportunity to really do well by their families to not consider my own legacy and to do something about it.

Reflection

1. What is the value of a plan? Consider your plan for your family and your family's legacy. And don't worry if you're not married or in a unique circumstance. We all leave a legacy of some sort. What I want you to consider is whether you have a plan for it.
2. Now that you've thought about plans generally and your own plan specifically, reflect on the elements to include in your vision for your legacy. What do you want to emphasize? When you're gone, what imprint do you want to leave on the world? What imprint do you feel God wants you to leave?
3. Consider what will happen at your death and at the death of your spouse. Are there issues that will lead to division in your family, whether unresolved conflicts or money matters? How can those be resolved now?

Discussion

1. Share your plans with each other. Go on, it's okay. If you don't have one, then share how you'd like to make a plan, and then brainstorm with your small group about some elements that would make sense in your plan.
2. Discuss the difference between how Israel blessed his twelve children and how Isaac treated Jacob and Esau. Was there a reason for the differences? Was one method better than the other?
3. Do you think that children should always be treated equally? Discuss the difference between fair treatment and equal treatment.

Chapter 11: Staying Rich

What is it that lasts in this world? That question drives my passion for writing this book. My mother always reminded me that only that which is done for eternal purposes will last, and that's usually the stuff you don't—can't—see. Our dreams, our work, our careers, all these things matter, but they are not the end of all that matters.

I firmly believe we all need to live, work, and play with a heavenly perspective. We need to pursue the things that matter to God, not to man. If we live our lives trying to please man, we'll never be at peace. We'll always be striving for one more raise, one more promotion, one more award, one more whatever. It'll never end.

I don't know about you, but the freedom I've experienced in giving it all away is something I cherish. Sure, I realize that my work matters. Working hard for the glory of God is important. But unless I'm doing it for the right reasons, corruption is not far away. If I simply want to grow Hobby Lobby to be this huge company simply to pass a financial legacy on to my kids and grandkids, I've already given up what matters most.

But if my purposes for working are my love for God and to make this world a better place because it's *his* kingdom, then I can relax, build with the tools I've been given, and watch God grow it. If I'm building Hobby Lobby so that it can provide the gospel message to folks all over the world, then what else could I want?

Reflection

1. Why has God put you on this earth? Have you really thought about it? To what end? Why this job? Why that opportunity?
2. We were created to work, to cultivate the world and its resources. God is a worker and a creator. We were made in his likeness. We're hardwired for work and creativity. But when

work and creativity become the goal, things can quickly go sideways. In what ways are you safeguarding your career and legacy from the dark side of ambition?

3. What does it mean for you to do things with an eternal perspective? How will that reality change the way you go about your day-to-day activities?

Discussion

1. What does it mean to live with an eternal mindset? Share your thoughts with friends and either discuss how this concept challenged you to rethink some things, or share how you do this already and suggest some tips that might help others.
2. List the things you'd like for your children and grandchildren to possess and pass on even five generations from now. How will you pass those items to them?
3. When you consider your life today, what are the things and people that you are invested in that will last for eternity?

Chapter 12: For Such a Time as This

The time for action is now.

When I say "get it all back again," you realize that I'm not talking about financial gain. I don't believe God honors a person who gives their money or their time to gain something financially. That's not to say he won't bless your finances ever. He's God, and he can do what he wants. But I don't think the person who gives in this way is pursuing the heart of God.

We give because he gave—he gave everything he had. That's the heart of God—it's a letting go of everything the world thinks is important for something of far greater worth.

Giving it all away is a posture. It's an attitude I want to pass on to my children and grandchildren. It's the one thing I hope folks remember me for. Not for anything I did. But that I pursued the heart of God even when it meant giving up what the world values most.

Reflection

1. Do you agree that we need a sense of urgency about setting up the next generation for success? Why or why not?
2. What do you think about this notion of giving everything away to get it all back again? Do you think it's a posture that can change each of us for the good, which will in turn change our culture, and even the world? Why or why not?
3. I started my career with three goals, and then expanded to five. I've now included "seeing our grandchildren and great-grandchildren serve God" and "to use our resources to tell as many people about Christ as we can." What are your goals at this stage of life? How have they changed over time?

Discussion

1. Well, you've made it to the end! Great job, and thanks for reading. Discuss the message of the book. What did you like? What did you dislike? What could you add to what I'm saying?
2. Share your thoughts on this time right now. Is the time ripe for a change in our mentality when it comes to how generous we are with our wealth, as I've defined it? It's one thing to read a book that inspires you to do something. But it's quite another to follow through. You put the book on the shelf and pour some coffee and the phone rings. It's on to the next thing. What can you and I do to make change a priority in

our lives? How can we inspire others to follow us down this radical path of stewardship?

3. What does it mean to live in this wonderful country and be afforded the opportunities many of us have each day? We're privileged to live in a country where a person can work in his or her garage making picture frames and turn it into a billion-dollar industry. I feel blessed beyond belief! But you and I must ask, "How can I utilize this privilege for, first, the glory of God, and, second, the good of humanity?" How will you and your group try to run out of cards? What will you do tomorrow to begin this new life of Crazy Eights?

APPENDIX

Legacy Profiles

Overview

Our family believes that there are only two things that will last for eternity: God's Word and people's souls. For that reason, we've invested heavily in those ministries that are concerned with these things. Here are some thoughts about two endeavors we care deeply about. I share them with a great deal of encouragement for you the reader. Think long-term.

What investments will you make that will outlive you? Some of them may seem small, while others may seem quite large. Some of you are called to go to another country or to serve in a mission here in the United States. I want to encourage you not to ignore that nudge from God. Some are called simply to be great stewards of their family.

I'm reminded of the story of the man who was found digging rocks from a field. Every day a passerby saw the man doing the same thing—building a bigger pile of rocks. Finally, the passerby asked the man if he would ever plant in the field. The man replied, "No, but my grandchildren will."

The Museum of the Bible

It's always seemed a bit strange that the bestselling book in the world, the Bible, has never had a national museum. Think about it. The Bible is the most banned book, the most burned book, and the bestselling book. It has its history and its stories.

Even Richard Dawkins, a well-known atheist, has said, "A native speaker of English who has not read a word of the King James Bible is verging on the barbarian."

A *Time* magazine article noted the one hundred events that had the greatest impact in the previous millennium. At the top of the list was Gutenberg's printing of the Bible.

Few will question the impact of the Bible on so many facets of everyday human life: science, literature, work, law, medicine, fashion, art—the list goes on.

The Museum of the Bible will be in Washington, D.C., and will be located at 4th and D Street. It will be five blocks from the Capitol and two blocks from the Smithsonian National Air and Space Museum. It will have 450,000 square feet of exhibit space.

It will house collections from the Vatican and Israel—collections that have never been shared with any other museum in the world. The museum will have three central floors featuring:

1. The narrative of the Bible
2. The history of the Bible
3. The impact of the Bible

The museum will be home to a collection of more than forty thousand biblical artifacts but will also showcase some top technology. For instance, the museum will feature a "flyover experience," where a person can have the visual feel of flying over Washington, D.C., to see all the places where scripture is inscribed into buildings.

However, the museum will be nonsectarian in its approach. People of all faiths and even those of no faith will be able to enjoy being in the museum.

Our family has taken the lead to help support the Museum of the

Bible and drive its efforts forward. Our second son, Steve, serves as the chairman of the board. In addition to the museum, efforts to promote engagement with the Bible include traveling exhibits, a scholars program, and a Bible curriculum.

To learn more, please visit www.museumofthebible.org.

Every Tribe Every Nation

Today, there are more than one billion people living without the full story of God's Word in their own language. Imagine having a desire to learn about spiritual things but having no ability to hear or read the Bible because it is not available in your language.

It used to take more than forty years to complete a Bible translation. Under the old models, it would not have been until the year 2150 that work would have started to complete Bible translations in all languages.

A handful of key leaders, including my oldest son, Mart, asked whether there was a better way. We began support of a digital Bible called YouVersion, which is the largest online Bible app. However, YouVersion had access to a relatively small number of Bible translations.

Over time, we've seen a number of Bible agencies, such as American Bible Society, United Bible Societies, Biblica, and Wycliffe, make their translations available for usage in the YouVersion App.

Every Tribe Every Nation is a cooperative effort to do the following:

1. *Accelerate Translations.* Every Tribe Every Nation is speeding up the process of Bible translation by funding projects and coordinating translation efforts.
2. *Build a Trustworthy Library.* We've developed a Digital

Bible Library, which is a secure collection of high quality translations, media files, and tools for mission fields around the globe.

3. *Standardize Digital Content.* For the first time, content is being digitized in a uniform and systematic environment, which eliminates the confusion of different formats and platforms.
4. *Provide Content Where It's Needed.* Every Tribe Every Nation is accelerating the distribution of translations by partnering with ministries to make specific Bible versions and resources available.

For more information, visit www.everytribeeverynation.org.

A Final Note

The Museum of the Bible and Every Tribe Every Nation are just two examples of our investment in projects that have eternal value. Our hope is that you will be inspired to invest in even greater and more creative projects and efforts around the world.

ACKNOWLEDGMENTS

AFTER WRITING ANY BOOK, there are many acknowledgments that can and should be made. But starting on that list inevitably leads to forgetting to put someone on it. In this case, I want to acknowledge the hardworking management team of Hobby Lobby. We have a great leadership team that makes the business of Hobby Lobby work, but, equally important, these leaders are invested in the ministry work that we do.

These efforts do not stop with our management team. They go far beyond just our leadership team. The growth and success of Hobby Lobby can be attributed to the thousands of employees who go to work every single day, who work hard and help our customers "live a creative life!"

As with my first book, I'm forever indebted to my wife, Barbara, who decided to take a chance on a young man with a dream, and my children—Mart, Steve, and Darsee—who have been equally willing to join me in this adventure. And as I've learned, their success is supported by their great spouses—Diana, Jackie, and Stan. They believe in and support the big ideas of family, legacy, and generosity.

NOTES

1. Daniel 3:17.
2. Carolyn Rosenblatt, "Wealth Transfers: How to Reverse the 70% Failure Rate," *Forbes*, December 9, 2011, http://www.forbes.com/sites/carolynrosenblatt/2011/12/09/wealth-transfers-how-to-reverse-the-70-failure-rate/.
3. John C. Maxwell, *The Twenty-one Irrefutable Laws of Leadership: Follow Them and People Will Follow You* (Nashville: Thomas Nelson, 1998), 224.
4. James Hamblin, "What Is Obamacare?" *The Atlantic*, April 2, 2013, http://www.theatlantic.com/health/archive/2013/04/what-is-obamacare/274509/.
5. David Green, "Christian Companies Can't Bow to Sinful Mandate," *USA Today*, September 12, 2012, http://usatoday30.usatoday.com/news/opinion/forum/story/2012-09-12/hhs-mandate-birth-control-sue-hobby-lobby/57759226/1.
6. National Right to Life Educational Foundation, "Abortion Statistics: United States Data and Trends," NRLC, n.d., http://www.nrlc.org/uploads/factsheets/FS01AbortionintheUS.pdf.
7. Later, Peter told me this amazing story: "I had been working with experts for months trying to figure out how to keep the fines from applying to us. I used multiple law firms, outside consultants, and some of the best minds in the industry to help me with this. I had workshops, think-tank sessions, and spent many sleepless nights running all the traps. The fate of our company could depend on this. I could probably write an entire chapter about all the different options we came up with. If one option did not work, the next option would compromise the family's belief. It went on and on this way for months.

   "On Thursday, the 27th, the day Justice Sotomayor ruled against us, I had a meeting in the Executive Conference Room with the entire family, Generations 1, 2, and 3, to discuss what the ruling meant and what options we had. There was a lot of talk and cross-talk, but at some moment during these discussions, I had a vision. It was so fleeting that it came and went before I knew what had happened. This I do know: what ran through my head was an option to keep the fines from applying to us. One that no lawyer, no consultant, no expert had ever raised in the months and months I had been working on this. Because the family discussions that day were rather in-depth about the recent ruling and what the next steps would be, I just as quickly forgot about the 'vision.'

"Later that evening I was home talking with my wife about my day. These times were very stressful, so going home and talking to my wife was not only cathartic for me, it seemed that being away from the office freed my mind up to deeper thought, prayer, and meditation. It was during this conversation that I remembered about the 'vision' earlier in the day, though I still didn't know what it was about.

"I immediately stopped what I was saying to my wife and told her that I needed to figure out what this 'vision' was. I was really excited. Anxious. I knew in my heart it was something big. Something no one had ever discussed. I hurriedly went into my home office, found a pen and the first piece of paper I could get my hands on, the back of an envelope, and started writing this: 'What was I thinking in our meeting re our plan?'

"No sooner had I finished writing the last word than the following words were written: "Change the plan year." Eureka! Talk about a V-8 moment! This was like asking someone if they know where your eyeglasses are, and they say 'on top of your head!' The solution was so simple, so rudimentary, that nobody ever even mentioned it before this moment.

"There is no doubt in my mind that God was just telling me to relax and allow him to be in charge. I'm not smart enough to have come up with this. When I let go and let God, he answered the question for me. To this day, I still keep that envelope as a humble reminder that when I seek his voice, he will answer my prayers."

8. When the case was filed, the case was known as *Hobby Lobby Stores, Inc. v. Kathleen Sebelius as Secretary of HHS*. Because we won at the tenth circuit and the government had to appeal, the order was reversed and the case became *Sebelius v. Hobby Lobby Stores, Inc.* During the Supreme Court procedures, Kathleen Sebelius resigned as secretary of HHS, and she was replaced by Sylvia Burwell. Thus, the case is now known as *Burwell v. Hobby Lobby*.
9. Randy Alcorn, *The Treasure Principle* (Sisters, Ore.: Multnomah, 2001), 13–15.
10. "Giving Research," Empty Tomb, Inc., n.d., http://www.emptytomb.org/fig1_07.html.

11. Chip Ingram, *The Genius of Generosity* (Generous Church, 2011), 24.
12. William F. High, "Short-Term Recession or the Long Winter? Rethinking the Theology of Money," *Christian Research Journal* 33, no. 1 (2010): 7.
13. David Wills, Terry Parker, and Greg Sperry, *Family. Money.: Five Questions Every Family Should Ask about Wealth* (Alpharetta, Ga.: National Christian Foundation, 2011), 60, https://www.nationalchristian.com/download/458.
14. The following language is in the Green Stewardship Trust that deals with compensation of family members who work for the company:

    "The Settlors believe that any such Green Family Member or spouse should be adequately and fairly compensated, but that compensation should not exceed what is fair and reasonable. Therefore, the Trustees shall cause each of the Green Family Companies to adopt policies and procedures that provide that any Green Family Member or spouse of a Green Family Member who is an employee or other service provider to any Green Family Company shall receive compensation and benefits which are fair and reasonable, but which do not exceed one and one-half times (1.5x) the amount of compensation and benefits which persons performing comparable services at the Green Family Companies would be entitled to receive and if there are no comparable positions at the Green Family Companies, then not to exceed one and one-half times (1.5x) the amount of compensation and benefits which those persons would otherwise be entitled to receive if they performed comparable services with other companies of comparable size anywhere in the United States."
15. Family Business Institute, Inc., "Family Business in Transition: Data and Analysis," part 1, January 2007, 2, http://ourfamilybusinesscrisis.com/images/fbi/resources/whitepapers/wp_fam_bus_in_transition_part_1.pdf.
16. Cited in Alcorn, *The Treasure Principle*, 70.
17. Wills, Parker, and Sperry, *Family. Money.* 37.
18. Ibid., 19.
19. Alcorn, *The Treasure Principle*, 85.
20. Wills, Parker, and Sperry, *Family. Money.* 29.
21. Thanks to Randy Alcorn for this illustration.
22. Alcorn, *The Treasure Principle*, 19.